THE
MODERN
TABLE

KIM KUSHNER

FOREWORD BY
ADEENA SUSSMAN

THE MODERN TABLE

Kosher Recipes for
Everyday Gatherings

Figure.1
Vancouver / Toronto / Berkeley

Cataloguing data is available from Library and Archives Canada
ISBN 978-1-77327-166-8 (hbk.)

Design by Naomi MacDougall
Photography by Kate Sears
Food styling by Hadas Smirnoff
Prop styling by Paige Hicks

Editing by Michelle Meade
Copy editing by Linda Pruessen
Proofreading by Breanne MacDonald
Indexing by Iva Cheung

Printed and bound in China by C&C Offset Printing Co.
Distributed internationally by Publishers Group West

Figure 1 Publishing Inc.
Vancouver BC Canada
www.figure1publishing.com

RECIPE NOTES

UNLESS STATED
OTHERWISE

Butter is unsalted.

Citrus juices are freshly
squeezed.

Eggs are large.

Flour is all-purpose.

Herbs are fresh.

Milk is whole.

Pepper is black and
freshly ground.

Produce is medium-sized.

Sugar is granulated.

For my sisters,
Heidi and Jordana

CONTENTS

10 FOREWORD

13 INTRODUCTION

19 ENTERTAINING

54 MENUS

97 GOURMET GIFTS

150 LEFTOVER MAKEOVER

RECIPES

33 STARTERS AND SOUPS

34 Vegetable Soup with Shaved Parmesan

35 Quick Ginger-Scallion Soup with Mushrooms and Chiles

36 Leek and Butternut Squash Soup (a.k.a. the Easiest Soup Ever)

38 Quick Golden Chicken Soup

39 Crudités on Ice with Flaked Salt

40 Honeydew with Sea Salt and Lime–Poppy Seed Drizzle

42 Spicy Tuna Tartare in Roasted Seaweed Cones

44 Spicy Green Tahini

46 Quick Pickled Vegetable Chips

48 Whipped Chive Ricotta with Truffle Honey and Grilled Sourdough

51 Mini Poke Bowls with Soy-Garlic Sauce

52 Roasted Almonds with Lemon and Thyme

61 SIMPLE SALADS

62 Arugula Salad, Black Olives, Black Sesame, and Citrus

63 Tomato Carpaccio with Iceberg Lettuce, Basil, and Balsamic Glaze

64 Grilled Peaches with Burrata, Basil, and Mint

66 Baby Gem with Pistachio Crumbs, Grainy Dijon, and Rose Petals

68 Frisée, Radicchio, Charred Broccoli, and Jammy Eggs with Creamy Dill Dressing

69 Petite Green Salad with Spicy Green Tahini

70 Herb Salad, Lime, Almonds, and Currants

72 Fennel, Pomegranate, and Parsley with Lemon-Za'atar Dressing

74 Kale and Chickpea Salad with Crunchy Curry Dressing

76 Cabbage, Cilantro, Salted Cashews, and Crunchy Chili Oil

FISH

79

80 Seared Salmon Bites with Jalapeño and Ponzu

82 Tuna Crudo with Radish, Citrus Zest, and Shallot

83 Crispy-Skinned Salmon

84 Smoked Salmon with Shallot, Dill, and Lemon

86 Sesame-Scallion Salmon Cakes

87 Grilled Halibut with Marinated Onions

88 Branzino with Lemon, Thyme, and Garlic

90 15-Minute Herb-Crumbed Fish

92 Fried Grey Sole with Lemon and Tartar Sauce

93 Sea Bass with Turmeric, Carrot, and Chickpeas

94 Arctic Char with Chili, Hazelnut, and Dill Oil

MEAT AND POULTRY

101

102 Garlic-Confit Chicken with Lemon and Thyme

105 Crispy Chicken with Herbs and White Wine

106 Chicken with Artichokes and Fennel

108 Chicken with Red Onion and Fig Sauce

109 Lemon-Pesto Chicken with Potatoes and Red Onions

110 Bibimbap

113 Classic Kosher Turkey

116 Steak with Scallions, Sesame, and Mint

117 Perfect Coffee-Rubbed Roast

118 Slow-Cooked Lollipop Short Ribs

120 Beef Kefta with Edamame and English Peas

122 Veal Milanese with Lemon and Arugula

125 Shawarma Salad with Za'atar Croutons and Tahini

126 Lamb Chops with Citrus and Sage

129 VEGETABLES AND SIDES

130 Crispy Mushroom Rice

131 Crispy Potatoes and Onions

132 Vegetable Ramen with Soy-Garlic Sauce and Peanuts

134 Baby Yams with Saffron Cream

136 Fried Eggplant and Jammy Eggs with Herb Oil

139 Slow-Cooked Caramelized Fennel

140 Za'atar Cauliflower Steaks

142 Charred Broccoli and Garlic

144 Asparagus with Eggs, Truffle Oil, and Parmesan

146 Hash Browns and Eggs

147 Mashed Potatoes with Onion Crème

148 Leek, Lentil, and Chickpea Tagine

155 SWEETS

156 Sliced Citrus with Pistachio Dust

158 Wine, Berries, and Chocolate

159 Berry Frosé

160 Moroccan Anise and Sesame Tea Biscuits

162 Chewy and Nutty Flourless Chocolate Chip Cookies

163 Quick Fruit Crisp with Oats and Cinnamon

164 Lemon–Poppy Seed Swirl Cake

166 Caramel Apple Pie on a Plate

168 Orange Blossom Chiffon Cake with Rose Petals

172 Israeli-Style Cheesecake

174 Chocolate Hazelnut Celebration Cake

176 METRIC CONVERSION CHART

179 ACKNOWLEDGMENTS

180 INDEX

192 ABOUT THE AUTHOR

FOREWORD

True story: The first time I met Kim Kushner, she came with snacks. But really, really special ones. After a lot of friendly Insta-chatter over several years, we arranged to meet at a spice market near my home in Tel Aviv. Kim walked up, somehow schvitz-free and cucumber-cool during peak hothouse Middle Eastern summer, and after serving up the warmest of hugs, she presented me with an oversized glass jar filled with her world-famous, wafer-thin fig biscotti from her first book, *The Modern Menu*.

Um, do I need to tell you it was love at first sight?

Years later, our friendship has deepened—a camaraderie anchored in all things edible, in a shared desire to feed souls by feeding people, and in an understanding of the power of cooking as a way to gather, to unify, to inspire, to share. I have spent time with Kim in the two countries I call home, and I always come away knowing myself better. It only recently dawned on me why.

It's because Kim knows exactly who she is, and that encourages us to know ourselves better, as cooks and as people. Wildly creative, incredibly grounded, culinarily gifted, fiercely family-first, quietly strong, willing to laugh at the world and herself—these are all powerful parts of Kim, and all elements of her essence that lend something special to her approach to cooking.

A stabilizing force for anyone she comes across, Kim is a cheerleader in the kitchen in ways we all need now more than ever. There's a lot of substance, with minimal fluff, an authenticity that comes through very clearly in her kitchen—an "aha" moment that, yes, a fancy rack of lamb might be nice, too, but if a plate of perfectly ripe honeydew melon dusted with sea salt and chili is enough, then it's enough for us as well.

There are lots of good cooks out there, but Kim… Kim just has that something extra. It's an élan she clearly was born with (but we can, with her help, learn); a grace that can't be taught (but maybe we'll absorb some by spending time within these pages); a generosity picked up at the side of her Moroccan mother's legendary hospitality; a table she so lovingly describes as an object lesson in kindness, in openness, in celebration. Kim took all of this and filtered it through the lens of her thoroughly modern life—and now we get a front-row seat into how she makes it happen. Don't you feel lucky?

Kim's style of cooking is lyrical yet practical, visually stunning but always focused on taste. Is it *amazing?* If not, don't bother! That's her way, and it's the right way. It's a path marked by colorful, comfortable cuisine that makes us feel hugged. The clear-eyed, easy-to-follow recipe writing and drop-dead visual presentation are part and parcel of all her cookbooks.

And, most importantly, she sets us up for success, for the end result—a perfect dish that delivers as promised in looks, taste, and satisfaction. Kim makes entertaining not only possible but enjoyable.

She also makes us better cooks because she lets us each see ourselves in her food. She makes sure we know that we have everything we need to pull off a killer meal, most often without a million fussy ingredients, overly complex recipes, or an excessive amount of hands-on time. A pot of braised ribs, a seasonal salad of fennel and pomegranate, a charming bottle of infused vodka, or a jar of honey-soaked fruit to gift to a loved one. We can do this! It can be pretty! It will be delicious! This is always how I feel after reading and cooking from *any* of Kim's books, but especially this one. As the world continues to emerge from isolation, this book practically begs us to gather around the table.

Kim shows us that whether it's a simple snack of salted almonds to share with unexpected guests; a sharing-sized platter of herb-topped fish to nourish our parents; or a slice of warm caramel apple pie to spoil the kids—it's all in the service of togetherness. This comes through clearly and confidently at every turn.

What I know above all else is that everything Kim does comes from a place of love. Love for family, love for friends, love for food. It seems effortless because Kim is effort*ful*. She's always thinking about us and how we will feel making a dish, how our guests or families will feel when seeing a stunning tablescape or a bunch of herbs whimsically fashioned into a centerpiece. There is intention without pretension, a natural inclination to make those eating or cooking feel loved, cared for, embraced.

In this gorgeous book you will find the bright, clean, beautiful, modern meals you've been looking for and will be making for years to come. Kim pours so much of herself into it all, and she's there with us on every page. But the true beauty of cooking with Kim is that she leaves so much room for each of us, too. Room to shine, to impress, to revel in the simple pleasures of a shared table. It's very decidedly her book, but now it's yours, too. All you have left to do is enjoy.

ADEENA SUSSMAN

INTRODUCTION

FOOD IS LOVE

I spend a lot of time thinking about food. When I wake up in the morning, my first thought is usually about that evening's dinner; when I tuck into bed at night, I'm already envisioning my steaming cup of morning coffee. In between, I devote my spare hours to reading food magazines, testing out recipes, researching flavor profiles, or discovering why friends and family enjoy their favorite dishes. As a result, my life is full of inspiration and creativity—all from food.

The power to transform just a few ingredients into something memorable has always been magical to me. Whether I'm making a simple and light herb salad (p. 70), a veal Milanese (p. 122) for a special occasion, or my signature lemon–poppy seed swirl cake (p. 164), I thoroughly enjoy the cooking process. I love seeking out the best quality ingredients, prepping them with consideration, and cooking attentively—which can be a visceral experience, full of color, sounds, flavors, and aromas to entice the senses. Few things bring me more joy than putting beautiful, delicious, and enticing dishes on the table for my family to enjoy.

Over the years (with time, age, and a little wistful reflection), I've come to realize that food is so much more than what we see on our plates. Don't get me wrong, *I love good food*. I love sinking my teeth into pure deliciousness, from creamy pasta dishes to crusty buttered slices of bread. But when I think about the best meals I've ever eaten, they always bring back memories of sitting around a table with wonderful people, laughing, learning, and loving.

I love the expression "breaking bread." Cooking for others is an opportunity to express kindness and generosity in the humblest ways. Still, the act of gathering around a table—a seemingly mundane action—bears far more significant meaning, because it offers moments for making connections. Whether you're sharing anecdotes about everyday happenings, engaging in gregarious banter, discussing current affairs, or just having a good laugh, these times of togetherness help nurture bonds and strengthen kinships.

I grew up in a home where, night after night, my Moroccan-born mother would welcome people into our home to join us at our dinner table. Some were familiar, but often they were new friends, neighbors, or acquaintances who would otherwise have been alone. On countless occasions, my mother would be the first to acknowledge, "They have nowhere to go." She's always had a generous heart, an inclusive spirit, and the wisdom to recognize the values of coming together. For her, memory-making with friends, family, and those within our community was an everyday occurrence. My younger self didn't quite understand her immense kindness to give so freely and openly to strangers. She would explain, "When there's room in the heart, there's room in the home." Unbeknownst to either of us at the time, those experiences would leave a deeply rooted impression and instill in me a desire to foster community. I am truly grateful for this.

I've adopted the same love for bringing people together and desire to create memorable meals that leave lasting impressions. Whether it's a casual midweek dinner or a full-on Shabbat feast (p. 55) with a broader group of friends and family, my goal is to make every get-together special.

In my mind, the dining experience is as much about the food as the feelings you express and experience. *The Modern Table* fuses my passion for simple, beautiful cooking, bringing people together, and entertaining. This book is all about togetherness.

I wanted to feature a collection of everyday and special occasion recipes that I prepare for those I love. The recipe collection features delicious, colorful, and flavorful Mediterranean-style recipes that define my cooking style and how we eat at home. It includes quick and healthy dishes such as Honeydew with Sea Salt and Lime–Poppy Seed Drizzle (p. 40) and Leek and Butternut Squash Soup (p. 36) that can be made with just a few easy-to-find ingredients. In addition, I love working with the bounties of the season: fresh, vibrant salads such as Grilled Peaches with Burrata, Basil, and Mint (p. 64) remind us of summer's best offerings. In contrast, a Quick Fruit Crisp with Oats and Cinnamon (p. 163) provides comfort when the temperatures drop. For a more substantial option, the delectable Slow-Cooked Lollipop Short Ribs (p. 118) rival some of my favorite restaurant dishes.

Our schedules are busier than ever before. So, when I'm short on time, I rely on a few quick and simple dishes that can be prepped, cooked, and on the table in a heartbeat. For this reason, recipes such as 15-Minute Herb-Crumbed Fish (p. 90) and Hash Browns and Eggs (p. 146) are on heavy rotation, often enjoyed with and accompanied by enthusiastic chatter about the events (and non-events) of the day.

It was also important to capture my culture through my recipes. My heritage is Moroccan and Ashkenazi Canadian, but I am an American woman living in New York City (I know, it's complicated). Therefore, I've included my Spicy Green Tahini (p. 44), which makes a fresh and bright accompaniment for crudités; my Insta-famous Za'atar Cauliflower Steaks (p. 140); and the insanely flavorful Leek, Lentil, and Chickpea Tagine (p. 148). The Orange Blossom Chiffon Cake with Rose Petals (p. 168), with its unrivaled fragrance, is a highlight when it comes to desserts. In keeping with my Moroccan traditions, I often corral guests into the living room for post-prandial conversations, mint tea, and anise and sesame biscuits known as *rifat* (Moroccan Anise and Sesame Tea Biscuits, p. 160). These recipes evoke so many fond memories and have become modern expressions of my heritage and cultural identity.

As with my previous cookbooks—*The Modern Menu, The New Kosher,* and *I "Heart" Kosher*— *The Modern Table* presents kosher cuisine in a fresh, contemporary light. Oftentimes, kosher cuisine can be confused with Jewish cuisine (think bagels and pastrami), but it refers to a dietary restriction, like vegan or gluten-free. So, when I speak about "kosher food," I'm referring to food that adheres to the biblical dietary laws of *kashrut*. Although kosher law does call for some limitations (for example, no pork, shellfish, or mixing of meat and dairy), my goal has always been to create delicious, fresh, seasonal, beautiful dishes that also happen to be kosher.

But remember, delicious food is just part of the equation. While I love preparing elegant dishes, I also enjoy creating an inviting and convivial experience for myself and my guests. So, in addition to the recipe collection, I've included inspirations for informal and formal menus (p. 54), simple floral inspirations (p. 22), and culinary gifts (p. 97). After all, nothing says "I love you" like a homemade edible treat. You'll even find great ideas for children's parties (p. 26).

The book also features tips for layering a gorgeous dining table. From dishware and table linens to flowers and décor, mixing and matching family heirlooms with bargain finds may be a departure from conventional style, but these items can come together to create exciting new looks. Likewise, everyday items you're likely to have at home—flowers, herbs, and inexpensive tchotchkes—can originate beautifully bespoke table settings. We really do eat with our eyes first, and I believe that this applies both to the food itself and the dining experience.

And let's be clear, a "dining experience" doesn't necessarily mean the dining table. Sure, it's the most likely choice, but you can share a meal just about anywhere: the kitchen, the dining room, the backyard, a local park, or even your workplace. The central idea is to bring people together.

Our family has a busy schedule. With work commitments, sports practices, and after-school activities, we can't eat together every night. But the three to four nights each week when the entire family—me, my husband, and our four children—shows up at the table, something magical happens. Phones are set aside, we engage with one another, we come together as a unit. All of us. These are times when my husband and I discover the most about our children and witness their astounding development. It could be a newly acquired skill, an interaction with the world, a perspective on a global matter. These seemingly inconsequential moments of food, casual observations, and musings (and the

occasional ribbing amongst the children) are treasured recordings, for me, of time and place. And I cherish these gatherings most.

So when it comes to cooking for larger groups, it was essential to include recipes that don't require much fuss. I always consider a balanced menu with something for everyone. This might consist of Vegetable Ramen with Soy-Garlic Sauce and Peanuts (p. 132) for vegetarians, Grilled Halibut with Marinated Onions (p. 87) for our pescatarians, or even Beef Kefta with Edamame and English Peas (p. 120) for the little ones. You may even find inspiration or ideas for your own table with the menus on p. 54.

HOW TO USE THIS BOOK

It has been a long-time dream to create a cookbook that speaks to these moments and encapsulates my views around food. Food at its essence is sustenance and a means for survival, yet it has a far greater power beyond nourishing bodies. When enjoyed with others, it can nurture relationships and bridge spaces for connection. These food expressions have been percolating in my mind for many years, so it is a great honor to share them with you. And to ensure kitchen success, I follow a few cardinal rules.

START WITH THE BEST INGREDIENTS.

I encourage you to prepare dishes in season, so you're working with optimal produce packed with maximum flavor and nutrients. Where possible, I prefer organic ingredients—this goes for produce, dairy products, eggs, and meat/seafood. When it comes to pantry staples, invest in high-quality products. For example, a high-quality extra-virgin olive oil should have a bright, earthy, and grassy smell and taste—not greasy or flavorless. Good dark chocolate is generally artisanal, locally produced, and naturally derived. It should also contain at least 70% cocoa. There are varieties of flaked salt (also known as finishing salt) that can have rough, flat, or spiky crystals and release their saltiness in a very delicious way. Explore the options and determine your favorites.

REVIEW THE RECIPE.

Before you start *any* cooking, I highly recommend reviewing the ingredient list and any relevant tips. These offer helpful advice and handy tips for special equipment, advanced preparation, omissions, substitutions, freezing, storage, and reheating—all to help navigate readers through the cooking process. (Think of it as my voice guiding you as you cook in the kitchen.) This way, you'll always be prepared for every step within the method instructions.

STAY ORGANIZED.

I don't know about you, but I appreciate the cooking process most when I am calm, organized, and prepared. If you're stressed out over the cooking, chances are you won't enjoy the process. So relax, put on a good playlist, and pour yourself a glass of wine. Have fun.

TAKE A FEW RISKS.

You are at liberty to change things around to make the recipe work for you (even if you're missing an ingredient or two). If the recipe calls for cilantro and you're not a fan or don't have any, feel free to replace it with parsley. If lemon isn't your favorite flavor, skip it altogether. Recipes are not written in stone. Imagine your recipe as a set of general guidelines and explore your creativity.

The preparation of food is a simple act of giving and showing others you care. Your time, food, and sentiment communicate an immeasurable expression of kindness, love, and gratitude. That is what food means to me. And maybe that's why it's always on my mind.

ENTERTAINING

When I invite my friends or family into my home, I feel like I'm welcoming them into my heart, my universe. I always want my guests to feel at ease. Our role as the host is to set the vibe for others, so I like to make it simple but significant.

Almost anyone can figure out how to throw a fancy party, but it takes more to throw a fun one! Fantastic food and drinks set the tone, and special touches such as bright flowers, personal elements, and a beautiful table setting can elevate the experience.

This section features my favorite ideas for hosting and creating memorable entertaining experiences. I'll show you how random items and trinkets from your home can introduce a personal decorative touch. Being prepared, organized, inspired, and creative will bring everything together.

DESIGN A TABLESCAPE

Whenever I set my table, I always start with a blank slate. The "building" of the table setting generally begins with a crisp tablecloth. From there, you can add objects to create a layered scene of color, textures, and visuals.

WILD AND FREE

Florals introduce color and texture to a table. Why buy lavish and elaborate bouquets when you can create a flourishing scene with fresh-cut flowers or herbs, such as basil or eucalyptus (as pictured) from the garden, or small plants in your home?

THE LIGHT REMAINS

Arrange candles of various types and heights to add visual interest and a stunning glow to the table. Try placing individual candles sporadically across your entire table or grouping them in bunches and setting them out on trays.

WHITE ON WHITE

No table setting is cleaner and crisper than simple white dishes on white table linen. This classic look never goes wrong and continues to be my go-to table setting time after time.

ODDS AND ENDS

Take advantage of glass jars and loose vessels occupying space (or cupboards!) around your home. Even simply colored bottles can make a great statement. You can add votive candles or decorative ornaments or fill the vessels with water and freshly cut flowers.

PERSONALIZE YOUR SPACE

Unique keepsakes and family heirlooms can mark a meaningful event. Family and guest photos can evoke deep sentiments and add a truly personal touch. You could even customize each place setting to the individual tastes or likes of each guest.

FRUITOPIA

Fresh fruit such as grapes, figs, cherries, and pomegranates can enhance the mood with deep colors. Instead of flowers, decorate the run of your table with fruit that looks beautiful and tastes delicious as well.

SERVING ELEMENTS

An inviting tablescape doesn't need to be complicated—a setting can be easily enhanced with a few additions of color and texture.

DIY GRAZING TABLE

Brown paper bags filled with a variety of nuts, dried fruit, or chips can decorate the table. Gently roll over the tops of the paper bags a few times until you reach your desired height. Sit them upright for a cleaner look or on their sides for a messier effect.

FLAVOR ENHANCERS

Small mezze-sized bowls such as the bases of terracotta pots can be used to serve up condiments and add some wow to your table. Fill these vessels with fresh chiles, preserved lemon, specialty salts, garlic confit, fried herbs (such as sage), or exotic spices like za'atar and dukkah.

DRINKWARE DONE DIFFERENTLY

Mix and match drinkware to create depth and uniqueness. This could mean a combination of drinking glasses, antique glassware, and that fancy crystal stemware you've tucked away. Then, put your favorites together on display for an eclectic touch.

DELIGHT IN THE LITTLE THINGS

To thank guests for their company, I like to present them with parting gifts to enjoy on their way home or the following day. Here, I've packaged truffles, fresh key limes, my favorite tequila, candied oranges, and nut bars. Alternatively, you could use your favorite store-bought goodies.

THE WILD BUNCH

Small bundles of flowers wrapped in twine double as décor and gifts for guests to-go. I love offering my guests something that they can take home at the end of the night, and a little bouquet goes a long way.

HERBS AND GREENS

Verdant displays of fresh herbs, leafy greens, and garden flowers enhance the simplest tablescapes. Instead of formal floral arrangements, look in the fridge for a bunch of leafy greens you may have on hand. Perhaps you can find some simple floral buds in your garden as well.

HAVE FUN, KIDS!

When it comes to children's parties, keep it playful and easy.

PAPER CONES

Serve freshly popped popcorn and potato chips in paper cones for easy clean-up. Line the table with a craft runner and provide lots of crayons and markers for doodling and birthday messages.

PICKY EATERS

Serve food in a fun way by using skewers and toothpicks, eliminating the oh-so-grown-up fork and knife! For example, you could skewer munchkins, mini pancakes, or even watermelon wedges.

SPRINKLES!

Everyone *loves* sprinkles. Decorate cakes, pies, or brownies with an array of fun sprinkles. Simply ice the dessert with your favorite frosting, use twine to divide sections on your cake, and fill in each section with a different sprinkle variety. Remove the twine, and voilà!

SUNDAE SERVICE

Here's a great reason to save all your fun plastic jars and reuse them! For pint-sized treats, fill jars with scoops of your favorite ice cream and add all the trimmings!

ACROSS THE BOARD

When I need to throw something together quickly and effortlessly for impromptu gatherings, I make a bountiful crowd-pleasing board. An impressive crudités board can be easily prepared with fresh vegetables and small bowls of your favorite dips, oils, or sauces. I also love creating beautiful dessert boards using store-bought pastry desserts and pairing them with cups of freshly steeped mint tea, chocolates, nuts, and fruit! These simple boards are perfect for grazing and bringing people together.

CRUDITÉS BOARD

Heirloom vegetables with stems and roots attached

Hummus

Flavored oils or high-quality extra-virgin olive oil

Tahini

Spicy mayo, spicy oils, or chili sauces

Chiles such as jalapeños, chili flakes in oil, Sichuan peppers, for garnish

Nuts

Olives

Slices of baguette or crackers

CHEESE BOARD

Cheeses

Grapes

Dried fruit

Nuts

Honeys

Preserves

Chocolate

BURGER BOARD

Burgers

Buns

Pickles

Onions

Tomatoes

Lettuce

Ketchup

Mustard

Mayo

Special sauces such as Russian dressing or chipotle mayo

Relish

BAGEL BOARD

Bagels

Cream cheeses

Tomatoes

Smoked salmon

Jammy Eggs (p. 136)

Persian cucumbers, halved lengthwise

Marinated onions

Capers

Lemon wedges

Bunch of dill

DESSERT BOARD

Cookies

Sliced cakes

Grapes, sliced figs, berries, or other fresh fruit

Individual fruit crisp, pastries, and tartlets

Chocolate

Cups of freshly steeped Moroccan tea or tea of your choice

CRUDITÉS BOARD

DESSERT BOARD

HOSTING

Friends and family often ask me why I seem so calm and relaxed as a host, and I attribute it to mastering the art of *enjoying* hosting. Of course, the process can be stressful and chaotic, but with a degree of pre-planning and forethought, you'll be able to enjoy the experience. Here are a few things I've learned over the years.

- **MOOD BOARD**. When I plan a party, I begin with building a mood board for how I imagine the day—the feeling, the vibe, the atmosphere. This often starts with the guest list, leading to the creation of the menu (for both food and drinks), ideas for table setting, personal touches, and memorable details.

- **STAY ORGANIZED**. People are often intimidated about hosting and overwhelmed by the process. However, you can be a relaxed/cool/chilled-out host by planning well, keeping things simple, and staying organized.

- **DO NOT OVERCOMPLICATE YOUR MENU**. Over the years, I've heard many horror stories of entertaining and testing out new recipes that created unnecessary stress and ended disastrously. Instead, select one or two familiar and manageable recipes that you can confidently prepare.

- **REMAIN COMFORTABLE**. Consider your set-up, décor, gifts, music, wine, and even wardrobe (need to be comfy all around) in advance. When you remove the pressure on yourself, things manage to fall into place.

STARTERS AND SOUPS

Feeding others is an act of intimacy. The healing effect of sharing food is a human effect, and all humans eat to survive. But it's the "sharing" of food that ultimately heals.

STYLING TIP

Florals introduce color and texture to a table. Why buy lavish and elaborate bouquets when you can create a flourishing scene with fresh-cut flowers or herbs, such as basil or eucalyptus (as pictured) from the garden, or small plants in your home?

This beautifully colored soup is so satisfying yet so simple to put together. Instead of a blender, I use a potato masher to "crush" the softened vegetables. This gives the soup a perfectly light consistency, and the shaved Parmesan adds a rich umami note.

A whole unpeeled onion in a soup or stock may seem like an unexpected addition, but it adds sweetness and a depth of golden color.

VEGETABLE SOUP WITH SHAVED PARMESAN

READY IN 35 MINUTES

SERVES 8

4 carrots, stemmed

1 small butternut squash, peeled, seeded, and cubed

1 yellow onion, unpeeled

1 yellow zucchini, stemmed and halved crosswise

1 large Garnet yam, halved

3 sprigs sage

2 quarts vegetable stock or water

1 Tbsp kosher salt, plus extra to season

½ tsp freshly ground black pepper

Shaved Parmesan cheese, for garnish

Chopped dill, for garnish

SPECIAL TOOLS OR EQUIPMENT
Potato masher

Combine carrots, squash, onion, zucchini, yam, and sage in a large saucepan. Pour in stock (or water) and stir in salt. Bring to a boil over high heat, then reduce heat to low and cook, uncovered, for 25–30 minutes, until vegetables can be easily pierced with a fork. Discard onion and sage.

Using a potato masher, mash vegetables until they are broken up and evenly crushed. Season with black pepper and more salt to taste.

Ladle soup into individual serving bowls and garnish each with shaved Parmesan and chopped dill.

OPTIONAL If you prefer a thicker soup, simply return the pan to the stovetop after the soup has been cooked and mashed. Bring to a boil, uncovered. Cook the soup for another 5–10 minutes on medium-high heat, stirring occasionally to check consistency, until thickened. Keep in mind that the soup will continue to thicken slightly as it cools down. This technique works to thicken all starchy soups and most sauces.

OMISSIONS To make the soup dairy-free, serve it without the Parmesan.

STORAGE Vegetable Soup, without the Parmesan, can be stored in the refrigerator for up to 1 week or the freezer for up to 3 months.

There is *no* replacement for chicken soup, but *really* good chicken soup can take hours to make. When we don't have the luxury of time, this fortifying soup requires only 30 minutes. The gingery-scallion flavors are light, soothing, and full of goodness.

QUICK GINGER-SCALLION SOUP WITH MUSHROOMS AND CHILES

1 bunch scallions, finely chopped (divided)

2 Tbsp toasted sesame oil

1 (3-inch) piece of ginger, peeled and julienned

2 cloves garlic, thinly sliced

2 cups sliced shiitake mushrooms

5 Tbsp soy sauce

2 quarts chicken or vegetable stock

2 baby bok choy, rinsed well and sliced lengthwise

Kosher salt and freshly ground black pepper

1 serrano chile, stemmed, seeded, and thinly sliced, for garnish

Set aside 2 tablespoons of scallions.

Heat sesame oil in a large saucepan over medium heat. Add the remaining scallions, ginger, and garlic. Cook for 3 minutes, until softened and golden. Add mushrooms and cook for another 5 minutes. Stir in soy sauce.

Pour the stock into the pan and bring to a boil. Add bok choy and reduce to medium-low heat. Simmer, uncovered, for 15 minutes. Season generously with salt and pepper.

Ladle soup into bowls, then garnish with the reserved scallions and sliced chiles.

OPTIONAL Add leftover shredded chicken for a hearty soup.

STORAGE The soup can be stored in the refrigerator for up to 5 days or the freezer for up to 3 months.

This autumnal soup bursts with warm, comforting flavors. The key is to blend the sweet, sautéed leeks with the creamy butternut squash. The result? A delicate, soothing, savory soup that is a major crowd-pleaser. If you're pressed for time, consider using store-bought cubed butternut squash.

LEEK AND BUTTERNUT SQUASH SOUP
(A.K.A. THE EASIEST SOUP EVER)

READY IN 1 HOUR

SERVES 8

2 Tbsp neutral oil such as avocado oil, vegetable oil, or rice bran oil

4 leeks, white and light green parts only, roughly chopped

1 butternut squash, peeled, seeded, and cubed

1 bunch thyme

2 quarts vegetable stock, chicken stock, or water

Kosher salt and freshly ground black pepper

Chili flakes, for sprinkling

Extra-virgin olive oil, for drizzling

Crusty bread, to serve

SPECIAL TOOLS OR EQUIPMENT
Cheesecloth (see tip below)

Kitchen twine

Heat oil in a large saucepan over medium heat. Add leeks and butternut squash and sauté for 10 minutes, stirring frequently, until leeks are browned and softened.

Wrap thyme in cheesecloth and tie it secure with kitchen twine. Pour in stock (or water) and add the bundled thyme. Bring to a boil, then reduce to medium heat. Cover and cook for 40 minutes, until the squash can be easily pierced with a fork. Discard thyme.

Using an immersion blender or a blender, purée soup until silky smooth. Season generously with salt and pepper.

Ladle soup into serving bowls. Sprinkle each with a pinch of chili flakes and a drizzle of extra-virgin olive oil. Serve with crusty bread on the side.

GET ORGANIZED Cheesecloth can be used to wrap fresh herbs into a bundle, known as a bouquet garni, which infuses flavor into soups, stocks, and braises without leaving behind any leafy remnants and makes it easy to remove.

OPTIONAL If you prefer a thicker soup, simply return the pan to the stovetop after the soup has been cooked. Bring to a boil, uncovered. Cook the soup for another 5–10 minutes on medium-high heat, stirring occasionally to check consistency, until thickened. Keep in mind that the soup will continue to thicken slightly as it cools down. This technique works to thicken all starchy soups and most sauces.

SUBSTITUTIONS The leeks can be replaced with chopped onions.

STORAGE The soup can be cooled, then stored in the refrigerator for 1 week or the freezer for 3 months.

The idea for this soup came from the belief that many healing minerals are found in vegetable skins. Root vegetables have many trace minerals from the soil, and vegetable peels are high in fiber and antioxidants and contain plenty of live pre- and probiotic bacteria from the environment.

My friend Alexandra introduced me to a recipe that uses vegetable skins to create a golden, nutrient-rich broth. I was amazed by the deep flavors and colors derived from the skins alone and adapted the recipe to make a quick and nourishing chicken soup.

QUICK GOLDEN CHICKEN SOUP

READY IN 40 MINUTES

SERVES 8

3 carrots, unpeeled

3 celery stalks and leaves

2 cloves garlic, unpeeled

1 large yellow onion, unpeeled

1 red potato, unpeeled

1 golden yam, unpeeled

1 bunch flat-leaf parsley

1 bay leaf

4 whole pink peppercorns

4 bone-in, skin-on chicken thighs

2 ½ quarts water

Kosher salt and freshly ground black pepper

Place vegetables and herbs in a large colander and rinse well under cold running water. Transfer vegetables, herbs, pink peppercorns, chicken, and water into a large saucepan.

Bring to a boil over medium-high heat. Reduce to medium heat and cook, uncovered, for 30 minutes. Using a slotted spoon or a spider strainer, remove chicken and set aside to cool slightly.

Using a fine-mesh strainer, strain the soup. Discard the vegetable and herb mixture.

Remove the chicken skin and bones. Using your hands, shred chicken and add to soup. Season with salt and pepper to taste.

SUBSTITUTIONS Use other unpeeled vegetables such as fennel, parsnip, turnip, and/or leeks.

STORAGE Quick Golden Chicken Soup can be cooled and stored in the refrigerator for up to 1 week or in the freezer for up to 3 months.

This dish concept was inspired by a crudité platter I had on a beach in Italy. Try incorporating a few unpredictable vegetables for your crudités and present them in a natural, rustic style—stems and roots attached for impact.

CRUDITÉS ON ICE WITH FLAKED SALT

READY IN 20 MINUTES

SERVES 8

1 fennel bulb, untrimmed

1 bunch rainbow carrots, untrimmed

1 bunch radishes, untrimmed

4 celery stalks, untrimmed

4 Persian cucumbers, unpeeled

2 endives

Ice cubes

2 Tbsp extra-virgin olive oil

½ tsp flaked sea salt

Quarter fennel lengthwise, removing the thick outer layer and keeping fronds intact.

Rinse carrots, radishes, celery, and cucumbers well under cold running water. Peel carrots, keeping stems or leaves intact. Cut lengthwise. Keep small radishes whole and halve larger radishes lengthwise. Halve celery lengthwise, keeping leaves intact. Trim cucumber stems, then slice cucumbers lengthwise.

Peel off endive leaves from the base, until you're left with the very center nub. Cut off the nub and discard the rough base. Using a damp paper towel, gently pat leaves clean.

Prepare a large bowl of ice water. Submerge fennel, carrots, radishes, celery, and cucumbers in the ice water for 10–15 seconds. Remove vegetables and pat dry with paper towels. Arrange them on a large platter or wooden board. Add the endive leaves. If preparing ahead of time, cover crudités with cold, damp paper towels and refrigerate for up to 3 hours.

Just before serving, grab a handful of ice cubes and scatter them over the vegetables. Drizzle with olive oil and sprinkle salt on top.

MAKE IT AHEAD Endive leaves, carrots, radishes, and celery can be cleaned, wrapped in paper towels, and stored in a zip-top bag in the refrigerator for up to 2 days.

Have you ever bitten into anything that made your taste buds explode? This is one of those recipes. I wouldn't ordinarily describe honeydew as memorable, but it does reach new levels when topped with a simple and adorned poppy seed. Remember to use honeydew in peak season or replace it with cantaloupe or watermelon.

HONEYDEW WITH SEA SALT AND LIME— POPPY SEED DRIZZLE

READY IN 10 MINUTES

SERVES 8

1 ripe honeydew melon
Juice of 2 limes (about ¼ cup)
1 tsp extra-virgin olive oil
1 tsp finely chopped mint leaves
½ tsp poppy seeds
Pinch of chili flakes (optional)
Flaked salt

Rinse and dry the outside of the melon. Using a large knife, cut melon in half across the center equator. Scoop out seeds and discard.

Place a melon half, flesh-side down, flat on a cutting board. Slice into wedges. Repeat with the other half. Transfer wedges onto a large serving platter and refrigerate until needed. (You can also place each wedge on its own individual salad plate, if you're serving formally.)

In a small bowl, whisk together lime juice, olive oil, mint, poppy seeds, and chili flakes, if using.

Just before serving, sprinkle each melon wedge with 2–3 salt flakes. Drizzle ½ teaspoon of sauce over each wedge and serve immediately.

MAKE IT AHEAD The melon can be sliced 1 day in advance and stored in the refrigerator.

MAKE IT AHEAD Lime–Poppy Seed Drizzle can be prepared up to 2 days in advance and stored in the refrigerator. Allow the sauce to come to room temperature before drizzling.

Tuna tartare is quick and easy to prepare, but I wanted a great way to serve it. One evening, as I was dicing the tuna, one of my kids ran by in the kitchen, munching away on crunchy, roasted seaweed. Then the idea dawned on me. Why not combine the two?! They're like miniature hand rolls from your favorite sushi place, only better.

SPICY TUNA TARTARE IN ROASTED SEAWEED CONES

READY IN 15 MINUTES

SERVES 4–6

SPICY MAYONNAISE
¼ cup mayonnaise
½ tsp Sriracha

CONES
1 (¾-lb) skinless and boneless sushi-grade tuna loin steak
2 Tbsp finely chopped scallions
1 Tbsp Spicy Mayonnaise (see here)
1 tsp toasted sesame oil
1 tsp everything bagel seasoning
Kosher salt and freshly ground black pepper
2–3 large sheets roasted seaweed (such as gimMe Organic)

SPICY MAYONNAISE Combine ingredients in a small bowl and set aside.

CONES Using a large knife, cut tuna into long, thin vertical strips (see tip below). Then cut the strips horizontally so you're left with ¼-inch cubes.

Transfer tuna into a glass bowl. Add scallions, spicy mayonnaise, sesame oil, and everything bagel seasoning. Gently toss to mix, taking care not to mash tuna. Season with salt and pepper to taste.

Cut a large sheet of roasted seaweed in half. Place a piece of seaweed in the palm of your hands, and then add about 2 tablespoons of tuna tartare into the center of the seaweed square. Wrap seaweed around tartare in a cone shape. To seal, use your index finger to dab a tiny bit of water along the edge of the seaweed wrapper to adhere the sides. Repeat with the remaining tuna and seaweed.

Serve immediately.

GOOD TO KNOW Spicy Tuna Tartare in Roasted Seaweed Cones should be assembled just before serving to ensure the seaweed stays crisp.

SUBSTITUTIONS Spicy mayonnaise is also readily available at most supermarkets or specialty food stores.

GET ORGANIZED When preparing raw fish, it's generally a good idea to wear disposable gloves and to try not to handle the fish too much. The less you touch the fish, the fresher it remains. Too much contact with your hands or a knife can alter the color, smell, and taste of the fish.

My husband and I can't get enough of this tahini. We douse it on fish, chicken, and meat—sometimes, we'll just dip crudités or crackers into it. It has the perfect amount of kick, but you can add the jalapeño seeds if you're looking for extra heat.

SPICY GREEN TAHINI

READY IN 5–10 MINUTES

SERVES 8

1 cup tahini (see tip below)

¾ cup water

1 clove garlic, peeled

1 jalapeño, stemmed and seeded, plus extra to garnish

½ cup chopped cilantro

Kosher salt and freshly ground black pepper

Crudités, to serve

SPECIAL TOOLS OR EQUIPMENT
Mini food processor (This is one of my favorite kitchen gadgets, and it's perfect for this recipe.)

Combine tahini, water, garlic, jalapeño, and cilantro in a food processor and process until smooth. Season generously with salt and pepper to taste. Garnish with chopped jalapeños and serve with crudités. That's all!

SUBSTITUTIONS Good news! If you despise cilantro, you can swap it out for basil or parsley—but really, cilantro is the way to go.

GOOD TO KNOW If your tahini separates, you can immerse the sealed jar in hot water for 2–3 minutes to loosen it up. (Alternatively, pop it in the microwave for a few seconds.) Then, shake it to mix.

STORAGE Spicy Green Tahini can be stored in an airtight container in the refrigerator for up to 1 week. Shake well before serving.

The best thing about this recipe is you can use ANY veggies so long as they have some bite. The amount of oil and vinegar is dependent on the quantity of veggies you'll be using. Generally speaking, the ratio should be two parts oil to one part vinegar. Add enough to cover the pickles halfway.

QUICK PICKLED VEGETABLE CHIPS

READY IN 15 MINUTES

SERVES 4–6

3 carrots, sliced into ¼-inch rounds

2 Persian cucumbers, sliced into ¼-inch rounds

1 red onion, thinly sliced

Handful of string beans, ends trimmed

1 small fennel bulb, thinly sliced

2 radishes, thinly sliced

¼–½ cup extra-virgin olive oil

2–3 Tbsp red wine vinegar

1 tsp dried oregano

½ tsp kosher salt

¼ tsp freshly ground black pepper

SPECIAL TOOLS OR EQUIPMENT
Large glass jar

Place vegetables into a large glass jar. Add olive oil, vinegar, oregano, salt, and pepper. (The vegetables should be submerged halfway.) Secure the lid tightly and shake well.

Set aside at room temperature for at least 10 minutes and up to 12 hours. (The longer the vegetables are left to marinate, the more flavorful they become.) Store in the refrigerator until needed.

GOOD TO KNOW Quick Pickled Vegetable Chips make great homemade gifts. Transfer the pickled veggies and pickling liquid into a Weck jar. Wrap the lid in a sheet of white parchment paper and wrap twine around the paper.

GOOD TO KNOW Add Quick Pickled Vegetable Chips over your favorite lettuce or greens for a fuss-free salad. No dressing necessary—just use the marinade in the jar.

STORAGE The chips can be refrigerated for up to 1 week.

This heavenly dish is ready on the table in 10 unbelievable minutes—which is perfect when you need a quick fix for guests. You can swap the sourdough for sliced baguette, grilled pita, or even your favorite crackers. I always keep a jar of truffle honey in my pantry. Just remember: a little goes a long way.

WHIPPED CHIVE RICOTTA WITH TRUFFLE HONEY AND GRILLED SOURDOUGH

READY IN 10 MINUTES

SERVES 8

1 (16-oz/454-g) tub whole milk ricotta cheese

1 Tbsp finely chopped chives, plus extra to garnish

Kosher salt and freshly ground black pepper

2 tsp truffle honey

1 Tbsp extra-virgin olive oil

1 loaf sourdough, cut into ½-inch-thick slices

SPECIAL TOOLS OR EQUIPMENT

Outdoor grill or indoor grill pan

Pastry brush

In a stand mixer fitted with the whisk attachment (or using a hand-held mixer), whip ricotta on high speed for 2 minutes, until fluffy. Using a spatula, gently fold in the chopped chives. Season with salt and pepper. Transfer to a serving bowl. Drizzle truffle honey over the whipped ricotta and garnish with chives.

Preheat an outdoor grill or indoor grill pan over medium-high heat. Brush olive oil on one side (or both) of the sourdough and grill for 1–2 minutes per side, until golden.

Serve the whipped chive ricotta with the grilled sourdough.

GOOD TO KNOW Sourdough is best grilled just before serving.

MAKE IT AHEAD Whipped Chive Ricotta can be covered and refrigerated for up to 4 hours. (Although the ricotta will be fluffiest just after whipping.)

Poke bowl night is a big thing in our home. If I announce that I'm serving roasted salmon and steamed rice for dinner, no one shows any excitement. Serve it in a bowl with lots of colorful toppings, though, and the meal suddenly springs to life and everyone's excited! You can also add leftover salmon or smoked salmon for another hit of protein.

MINI POKE BOWLS WITH SOY-GARLIC SAUCE

READY IN 10 MINUTES

SERVES 6

½ cup soy sauce

3 Tbsp apple cider vinegar

1 tsp honey

1 clove garlic, minced

2 Tbsp dark brown sugar

2 Tbsp toasted sesame oil

1 ½ cups cooked sushi rice, room temperature

1–2 lbs cooked salmon (roasted, poached, or grilled, skin and bones removed, and flaked with a fork)

8 oz imitation crab sticks (about 8), thawed and shredded (optional)

1 English cucumber, julienned

2 carrots, julienned

½ cup frozen shelled edamame, thawed and rinsed under cold water (see tip below)

2 Tbsp black and white sesame seeds

¼ cup finely chopped scallions

SPECIAL TOOLS OR EQUIPMENT

Julienne peeler

6 ramekins

In a small saucepan, combine soy sauce, apple cider vinegar, honey, garlic, and brown sugar and bring to a boil over high heat. Reduce to medium heat and cook for 3 minutes, until sugar has dissolved. Remove pan from heat and stir in sesame oil.

Place ¼ cup of sushi rice into each ramekin. Top with salmon, imitation crab, if using, cucumbers, carrots, edamame, sesame seeds, and scallions. Drizzle the sauce over each poke bowl.

GOOD TO KNOW Frozen edamame do not need to be cooked—I promise! Simply thaw at room temperature or overnight in your refrigerator and run under cold water before serving.

GOOD TO KNOW Sushi rice is best made just before serving.

MAKE IT AHEAD The toppings (imitation crab sticks, cucumber, carrots, edamame, and scallions) can be prepared in advance and stored in containers in the refrigerator for up to 2 days.

MAKE IT AHEAD Soy-Garlic Sauce can be made up to 2 days in advance. When ready to serve, reheat on the stovetop over low heat until warmed through.

Warm, salty, earthy almonds served with a glass of wine (or maybe something stronger) is my favorite evening snack combo! And roasting nuts at home is simpler than you might think. Always start with raw whole nuts, then roast them on a parchment-lined baking sheet and toss in oil while hot. Once you develop the confidence, try creating your own combinations.

ROASTED ALMONDS WITH LEMON AND THYME

READY IN 20–25 MINUTES

SERVES 6

2 tsp hot water
¾ tsp kosher salt
2 cups raw almonds
4 sprigs thyme, leaves only
Grated zest of 1 lemon
2 Tbsp extra-virgin olive oil

Preheat oven to 375°F. Line a baking sheet with parchment paper.

Combine water and salt in a medium bowl and stir until salt has dissolved. Add almonds and stir to coat. Mix in thyme and lemon zest.

Transfer almonds to the prepared baking sheet. Bake for 10 minutes, rotate pan, and bake for another 5–8 minutes, until fragrant. Transfer almonds to a bowl, add olive oil, and toss.

Serve warm or at room temperature.

VARIATIONS

These seasoned nuts deliver on taste, and making them couldn't be any easier. Simply use the same recipe and replace the nut or seasoning blend.

CASHEWS WITH ZA'ATAR AND BLACK PEPPER

1 Tbsp za'atar
¼ tsp coarsely ground black pepper

ALMONDS WITH SESAME SEEDS AND CHILI POWDER

1 Tbsp white sesame seeds
1 Tbsp black sesame seeds
1 Tbsp chili powder

MENUS

PERFECT FOR GATHERINGS

I love bringing friends and family together, engaging in dynamic conversations, and sharing my favorite foods with those around me. My only request is for guests to bring a healthy appetite and good banter!

BRUNCH

Herb Salad, Lime, Almonds, and Currants (p. 70)

Smoked Salmon with Shallot, Dill, and Lemon (p. 84)

Hash Browns and Eggs (p. 146)

Sliced Citrus with Pistachio Dust (p. 156)

Bagel Board (p. 28)

CINQ À SEPT

Roasted Almonds with Lemon and Thyme (p. 52)

Spicy Tuna Tartare in Roasted Seaweed Cones (p. 42)

Seared Salmon Bites with Jalapeño and Ponzu (p. 80)

Honeydew with Sea Salt and Lime–Poppy Seed Drizzle (p. 40)

Baby Yams with Saffron Cream (p. 134)

Whipped Chive Ricotta with Truffle Honey and Grilled Sourdough (p. 48)

WINTER LUNCH

Quick Ginger-Scallion Soup with Mushrooms and Chiles (p. 35)

Fennel, Pomegranate, and Parsley with Lemon-Za'atar Dressing (p. 72)

Garlic-Confit Chicken with Lemon and Thyme (p. 102)

Za'atar Cauliflower Steaks (p. 140)

Caramel Apple Pie on a Plate (p. 166)

Here are just a few of my favorite occasions and menus to prepare for others. When building a menu, I like to offer a variety of colorful and flavorful dishes that complement one another.

SPECIAL OCCASION

Baby Gem with Pistachio Crumbs, Grainy Dijon, and Rose Petals (p. 66)

Tuna Crudo with Radish, Citrus Zest, and Shallot (p. 82)

Slow-Cooked Lollipop Short Ribs (p. 118)

Crispy Potatoes and Onions (p. 131)

Orange Blossom Chiffon Cake with Rose Petals (p. 168)

SHABBAT DINNER

Quick Pickled Vegetable Chips (p. 46)

Spicy Green Tahini (p. 44)

Fried Eggplant and Jammy Eggs with Herb Oil (p. 136)

Cabbage, Cilantro, Salted Cashews, and Crunchy Chili Oil (p. 76)

Veal Milanese with Lemon and Arugula (p. 122)

Charred Broccoli and Garlic (p. 142)

Lemon–Poppy Seed Swirl Cake (p. 164)

OUTDOOR DINING

Crudités on Ice with Flaked Salt (p. 39)

Grilled Peaches with Burrata, Basil, and Mint (p. 64)

Arctic Char with Chili, Hazelnut, and Dill Oil (p. 94)

Crispy Mushroom Rice (p. 130)

Moroccan Anise and Sesame Tea Biscuits (p. 160)

Chocolate Hazelnut Celebration Cake (p. 174)

SHABBAT DINNER

SIMPLE SALADS

Less is more.
Go with tried and true
every time.

STYLING TIP

Unique keepsakes and family heirlooms can mark a meaningful event. Family and guest photos can evoke deep sentiments and add a truly personal touch. You could even customize each place setting to the individual tastes or likes of each guest.

This colorful salad with its peppery arugula, briny black olives, citrus orange, and crunchy black sesame is full of gusto. You can use any type of olive, but I love how much flavor is delivered with dry-cured black olives.

ARUGULA SALAD, BLACK OLIVES, BLACK SESAME, AND CITRUS

READY IN 15 MINUTES

SERVES 8

6 cups arugula

¼ cup pitted olives (I like dry-cured black Moroccan olives)

1 navel or blood orange

¼ cup extra-virgin olive oil

3 Tbsp red wine vinegar

1 Tbsp grainy Dijon

1 tsp date syrup or honey

1 Tbsp black sesame seeds

½ tsp kosher salt

¼ tsp freshly ground black pepper

In a large bowl, toss together arugula and olives.

Using a sharp paring knife, slice off the top and bottom of the orange, just enough to expose the flesh. Place orange, cut-side down, so that it is sturdy on your cutting board. Cut away as much of the peel and white pith as possible by following the orange's shape. Now, holding the fruit in one hand, carefully cut along each side of the membranes that separate the orange segments to free the segments (called "supremes"). Add the segments to the bowl and gently toss.

In a small bowl, whisk together olive oil, vinegar, grainy Dijon, date syrup (or honey), and sesame seeds. Drizzle the vinaigrette over the salad, then season with salt and pepper. Using your hands, toss together.

Serve immediately.

SUBSTITUTIONS Feel free to try this salad with any citrus variety.

MAKE IT AHEAD The arugula, olives, and orange can be stored in separate containers in the refrigerator up to 8 hours in advance.

STORAGE The vinaigrette can be stored in the refrigerator for up to 1 week.

This refreshing salad sees thinly sliced beefsteak tomato topped with crisp wedges of lettuce, aromatic basil, and a rich glaze to bring it all together. Learning to peel a tomato and mastering a balsamic glaze are useful skills to add to your repertoire.

TOMATO CARPACCIO WITH ICEBERG LETTUCE, BASIL, AND BALSAMIC GLAZE

READY IN 20 MINUTES

SERVES 8

BALSAMIC GLAZE

2 cups good-quality balsamic vinegar

½ cup brown sugar

SALAD

2 large beefsteak tomatoes

½ head iceberg lettuce, cut into 8 wedges

1 cup basil leaves

2 Tbsp extra-virgin olive oil

¼ tsp kosher salt

Freshly ground black pepper

2 Tbsp Balsamic Glaze (see here)

SPECIAL TOOLS OR EQUIPMENT

Mandolin (optional)

BALSAMIC GLAZE In a small saucepan, combine vinegar and sugar and bring to a gentle boil over medium heat. Simmer for 8–10 minutes, until thickened and reduced to ½ cup. Remove from heat and set aside to cool completely.

SALAD Prepare an ice bath.

Bring a saucepan of water to a boil. Using a sharp paring knife, remove tomato stems and discard. Score an "X" shape at the base of each tomato. Gently lower tomatoes into the boiling water and boil for 1 minute. Transfer the tomatoes to the ice bath and set aside for 1 minute. Once cool enough to handle, remove the skin starting from the base.

Using a mandolin or a chef's knife, thinly slice tomato rounds. Transfer tomato slices onto a serving platter. Arrange the lettuce wedges over the tomato.

Stack basil leaves and roll them into a cylinder. Using a chef's knife, thinly slice the basil. The tighter you roll the leaves, the frizzier they will turn out when sliced. Scatter basil over the salad, then drizzle with olive oil. Season with salt and pepper.

Drizzle balsamic glaze over the salad. Serve immediately.

STORAGE Leftover dressing can be stored in an airtight container in the refrigerator for 1 week.

With luscious, sweet, and creamy burrata, sweet juicy peaches, and fresh basil and mint, this salad sings of summer! Grilling peaches is a great way to release their juices and soften them ever so slightly. Serve salad with toasted sourdough bread and a glass of crisp white wine for an elegant warm-weather meal.

GRILLED PEACHES WITH BURRATA, BASIL, AND MINT

READY IN 15–20 MINUTES

SERVES 8

Cooking spray

4 ripe peaches, pitted and quartered

1 (8-oz) burrata, cut into 1-inch pieces

¼ cup basil leaves, torn into small pieces

4–5 mint leaves, cleaned, dried, and torn into small pieces

3 Tbsp extra-virgin olive oil

¼ tsp kosher salt

¼–½ tsp freshly ground black pepper

SPECIAL TOOLS OR EQUIPMENT

Outdoor grill or indoor grill pan

Preheat an outdoor grill or indoor grill pan over high heat. Spray with cooking spray, then add peaches, cut-side down. Grill for 5–7 minutes, rotating occasionally to ensure all sides are grilled.

Transfer peaches to a serving platter. Arrange burrata, then scatter basil and mint on top. Finish with a drizzle of olive oil and season with salt and pepper. Serve immediately.

GOOD TO KNOW Burrata is best served at room temperature. I usually take it out of the refrigerator 1 hour before cutting. And yes, you can eat its outer layer of "skin."

SUBSTITUTIONS If you can't find burrata, use dollops of ricotta or slices of fresh mozzarella.

SUBSTITUTIONS Peaches can be replaced with plums or nectarines.

If there's such a thing as a sexy salad, this might be it. Baby gem lettuce is a small lettuce variety that resembles a bite-sized version of romaine. Topped with brilliantly green pistachio-pesto crumbs and garnished with rose petals, this is a salad to make when you're looking to impress. And I mean impress yourself, not anyone else.

BABY GEM WITH PISTACHIO CRUMBS, GRAINY DIJON, AND ROSE PETALS

READY IN 15 MINUTES

SERVES 8

6 baby gem lettuces

½ cup plain breadcrumbs

½ cup basil leaves

¼ cup shelled unsalted pistachios

1 Tbsp grainy Dijon

3 Tbsp extra-virgin olive oil, plus extra for drizzling

½ tsp kosher salt, plus extra for sprinkling

¼ tsp freshly ground black pepper

1 tsp edible dried rose petals, crushed, for garnish (see tip below)

SPECIAL TOOLS OR EQUIPMENT
Food processor
Salad spinner (optional)

Slice baby gems in half lengthwise and rinse them under cold running water. Dry well with paper towels or in a salad spinner. Do not pull leaves apart—you want to keep the halves intact.

In a food processor, combine breadcrumbs, basil, pistachios, and grainy Dijon. Process until a paste forms. Add olive oil, salt, and pepper and process for another minute, until thoroughly combined.

Drizzle 1 tablespoon of olive oil on a serving platter. Sprinkle a pinch of salt on top. Arrange baby gems, cut-side up, on the platter. Spoon pistachio crumbs over the lettuce, then garnish with rose petals.

GOOD TO KNOW Edible rose petals are simply dried rose petals and are readily available online, in specialty food stores, and at most farmer's markets. Check the packaging for organically grown roses that are free of sprays and pesticides. And, keep in mind, a little bit goes a long way.

MAKE IT AHEAD The baby gem lettuce can be cleaned and dried, wrapped in paper towels, and stored in a plastic bag in the refrigerator for up to 1 week.

MAKE IT AHEAD The pistachio crumbs can be prepared 1 week in advance and stored in the refrigerator.

Frisée, also known as "curly endive," is readily available at most supermarkets, but it is often overlooked. Wild and seemingly unwieldy, this lacy lettuce has a great texture that stands up to thick and creamy dressings. It provides a great bite, offers the right amount of bitterness, and doesn't get soggy.

FRISÉE, RADICCHIO, CHARRED BROCCOLI, AND JAMMY EGGS WITH CREAMY DILL DRESSING

READY IN 20 MINUTES

SERVES 8

1 head frisée

1 small head radicchio

4 Jammy Eggs (p. 136)

1 cup chopped Charred Broccoli (p. 142)

1 cup plain full-fat Greek yogurt

3 Tbsp extra-virgin olive oil

1 Tbsp grainy Dijon

Juice of 1 lemon (about 3 Tbsp)

¼ cup finely chopped dill

¼ tsp kosher salt

Pinch of freshly ground black pepper

SPECIAL TOOLS OR EQUIPMENT

Mandolin (optional)

Salad spinner (optional)

Remove the large outer leaves of the frisée and discard. Using a large knife with a downward motion, shred the frisée. Rinse under cold running water, then dry well in a salad spinner or by wrapping it in a clean dish towel and wringing out all the moisture. Transfer onto a platter.

Using a mandolin or a chef's knife, shred radicchio as thinly as possible. Add to platter.

Halve eggs across the center. Arrange charred broccoli and eggs on top of the frisée and radicchio.

In a small bowl, whisk together yogurt, olive oil, grainy Dijon, lemon juice, dill, salt, and pepper until well combined.

Dollop the dressing over salad and serve immediately.

GOOD TO KNOW Radicchio browns quickly once cut. Shred it just before adding it to the salad.

MAKE IT AHEAD Washed and dried frisée can be wrapped in paper towels and stored in a plastic bag in the refrigerator for up to 4 days in advance.

This is a quick and easy salad to throw together (plus, you can finally use up that bag of peas in your freezer!). Salads are not meant to be too sweet, but I add a touch of sugar to mellow out the sharpness of the lemon juice. This precious salad can be served on its own or alongside grilled fish such as 15-Minute Herb-Crumbed Fish (p. 90) for a heartier meal.

PETITE GREEN SALAD WITH SPICY GREEN TAHINI

READY IN 15 MINUTES

SERVES 8

5 cups spinach, washed and dried

2 cups frozen peas, shelled and thawed (see tip below)

2 cups sugar snaps, trimmed and julienned

2 avocados, cut into ½-inch cubes

Juice of 1 lemon (about 3 Tbsp)

1 Tbsp extra-virgin olive oil

½ tsp sugar

¼ tsp kosher salt

Pinch of freshly ground black pepper

3 Tbsp Spicy Green Tahini (p. 44)

Using a chef's knife, roughly chop spinach. Transfer to a medium bowl or platter. Add peas, sugar snaps, and avocado and toss.

In a small bowl, combine lemon juice, olive oil, sugar, salt, and pepper. Pour over salad and gently toss. Drizzle tahini on top. Serve immediately.

GOOD TO KNOW Frozen peas do not need to be cooked—I promise! Simply thaw at room temperature or overnight in your refrigerator and run under cold water before serving.

MAKE IT AHEAD The spinach, peas, and sugar snaps can be prepared and assembled up to 5 hours in advance and stored in the refrigerator.

We have this misconception that a salad needs to include leafy greens, but I'm here to tell you otherwise. This salad is loaded with bright herbs, crunchy toasted almonds, and tart currants and served with a creamy yogurt dip. It's so delicious, I've been known to polish off the entire platter myself.

HERB SALAD, LIME, ALMONDS, AND CURRANTS

READY IN 20 MINUTES

SERVES 8

1 bunch flat-leaf parsley, leaves and stems finely chopped

1 bunch curly parsley or cilantro, leaves and stems finely chopped

1 bunch dill, leaves and stems finely chopped

1 bunch scallions, finely chopped

¼ cup mint leaves, finely chopped

¼ cup sliced almonds

¼ cup dried currants

¼ cup extra-virgin olive oil (divided)

Juice of 2 limes (about ¼ cup)

1 tsp kosher salt

¼ tsp freshly ground black pepper

¾ cup plain full-fat Greek yogurt

2 Tbsp za'atar

Combine herbs and scallions in a medium mixing bowl.

Heat a small nonstick skillet over medium heat. Add almonds and toast for 3 minutes on each side, until golden. Cool slightly.

Add almonds and currants to the bowl. Add 3 tablespoons of olive oil, lime juice, salt, and pepper. Using your hands, toss everything together.

Transfer the salad to a serving platter and make a well in the center. Dollop yogurt into the well, sprinkle with za'atar, and drizzle the remaining 1 tablespoon of oil on top. Serve immediately.

SPECIAL TOOLS OR EQUIPMENT
Salad spinner (see tip at right)

GET ORGANIZED I like to clean fresh, bunched herbs by using a salad spinner. Place herbs in the strainer basket and rinse under cold running water. (If you have a spray function, best to use that as it doesn't water down the herbs.) Transfer basket to the spinner and spin until the water has been extracted. Transfer herbs onto a dry dish towel, then wrap tightly. Place the toweled herbs into a plastic bag and store in the refrigerator for up to 1 week.

SUBSTITUTIONS Feel free to use other fresh leafy herbs such as basil.

MAKE IT AHEAD Sliced almonds can be toasted and stored in an airtight container for up to 2 months.

Few things in the culinary world annoy me more than to see parsley used only as a garnish at restaurants. (I always make a point of eating it!) Herbaceous parsley is a staple in my kitchen, often used to brighten a dish with clean, earthy flavor. In this crunchy salad, parsley lends a touch of freshness to balance out mellow fennel and tart pomegranate. It's a definite keeper.

FENNEL, POMEGRANATE, AND PARSLEY WITH LEMON-ZA'ATAR DRESSING

READY IN 15 MINUTES

SERVES 8

1 medium fennel bulb, trimmed, fronds reserved for garnish

1 cup flat-leaf parsley leaves, roughly chopped

¼ cup pomegranate seeds

Grated zest and juice of 1 lemon (about 3 Tbsp)

3 Tbsp extra-virgin olive oil

1 tsp grainy Dijon

1 tsp honey

2 Tbsp za'atar

¼ tsp kosher salt

Freshly ground black pepper

SPECIAL TOOLS OR EQUIPMENT
Mandolin (optional)

Using a mandolin or a large knife, thinly slice fennel. Transfer to a medium bowl or platter, then add parsley and pomegranate seeds.

In a small bowl, whisk together lemon zest and juice, olive oil, grainy Dijon, honey, za'atar, salt, and pepper.

Spoon dressing over salad and toss to mix. Garnish with the reserved fennel fronds and serve immediately.

MAKE IT AHEAD Undressed Fennel, Pomegranate, and Parsley Salad can be prepared in advance and stored in the refrigerator for up to 6 hours.

MAKE IT AHEAD Lemon-Za'atar Dressing can be prepared 1 week in advance and stored in the refrigerator.

The cucumber and chickpea marinade in this excellent winter salad eventually becomes the dressing, which seasons and softens the kale leaves. The textural contrast between the tangy curried chickpeas and the crunchy seeds is a delight to the palate.

KALE AND CHICKPEA SALAD WITH CRUNCHY CURRY DRESSING

READY IN 20 MINUTES

SERVES 8

1 bunch green kale, tough stems removed

2 Persian cucumbers, cut into thin rounds

1 (15-oz) can chickpeas, rinsed and drained

¼ cup extra-virgin olive oil

3 Tbsp rice vinegar

1 Tbsp yellow mustard

2 tsp honey

½ tsp curry powder

¼ tsp kosher salt

¼ tsp freshly ground black pepper

¼ cup roasted and salted sunflower seeds

Using a chef's knife, shred kale into very thin strips. Place kale in a large bowl.

In a medium bowl, combine cucumbers and chickpeas and toss.

In a small bowl, whisk together olive oil, vinegar, mustard, honey, curry powder, salt, and pepper. Pour dressing over the cucumbers and chickpeas. Set aside at room temperature to marinate for at least 10 minutes and up to 6 hours.

Pour the marinated cucumbers and chickpeas over the kale, add sunflower seeds, and toss well to combine. Serve immediately.

Can you handle the heat? I LOVE spicy food—and funny enough, all my favorite people in this world love spicy food too. Coincidence? A little heat and a hint of crunch perk up this hearty salad—it's a blast of flavor and texture with every mouthful.

CABBAGE, CILANTRO, SALTED CASHEWS, AND CRUNCHY CHILI OIL

READY IN 20 MINUTES

SERVES 8

4 cups shredded red cabbage

4 cups shredded green cabbage

¼ cup rice vinegar

2 tsp coconut sugar or brown sugar

½ tsp kosher salt

¼ tsp freshly ground black pepper

2 Tbsp neutral oil such as avocado oil, vegetable oil, or rice bran oil

1 clove garlic, minced

1 tsp chili flakes

¼ cup crushed roasted salted cashews

1 Tbsp roasted salted sunflower seeds

1 Tbsp roasted pumpkin seeds

1 Tbsp roasted sesame seeds

½ tsp toasted sesame oil

¼ cup cilantro leaves, roughly chopped

In a large bowl, combine cabbages, vinegar, and sugar. Season with salt and pepper. Using your hands, toss to combine. Set aside to marinate.

Meanwhile, heat neutral oil in a large nonstick skillet over medium-high heat. Add garlic, chili flakes, cashews, and seeds and sauté for 5 minutes, until golden. Transfer mixture to a small bowl, then stir in sesame oil.

Scatter cilantro over the cabbage. Drizzle with crunchy chili oil and toss well. Serve immediately.

GOOD TO KNOW You can double or triple the recipe for the crunchy chili oil. It is delicious on almost everything!

MAKE IT AHEAD The shredded cabbage can be marinated for up to 5 hours in the refrigerator.

STORAGE Crunchy Chili Oil can be stored in a glass jar in your pantry for up to 2 weeks.

FISH

Have fun and play around with your cooking. If you're stressed over cooking, chances are you won't enjoy it.

STYLING TIP

Arrange candles of various types and heights to add visual interest and a stunning glow to the table. Try placing individual candles sporadically across your entire table or grouping them in bunches and setting them out on trays.

Ponzu is a tart, citrusy sauce used in Japanese cooking. My version is slightly milder than the traditional sauce, but it works very well with the delicate, just-cooked salmon slices.

SEARED SALMON BITES WITH JALAPEÑO AND PONZU

READY IN 20 MINUTES

SERVES 6

PONZU SAUCE

Juice of 1 orange (about ¼ cup)

1 Tbsp mirin (sweet Japanese rice wine)

1 Tbsp soy sauce

1 Tbsp rice vinegar

1 tsp honey

¼ tsp toasted sesame oil

SEARED SALMON

2 (1-lb) skinless salmon fillets

Pinch of kosher salt

1 tsp light olive oil

ASSEMBLY

1 jalapeño, stemmed and thinly sliced

PONZU SAUCE In a small saucepan, combine orange juice, mirin, soy sauce, vinegar, and honey and bring to a boil. Reduce heat to medium and simmer for 4 minutes, or until sauce has thickened slightly. Set aside to cool. Stir in sesame oil.

SEARED SALMON Using a chef's knife, slice the fillets across the grain into ¼-inch-thick slices. Sprinkle with a pinch of salt.

Heat olive oil in a nonstick skillet over medium-high heat. Working in batches, add 6–8 salmon slices and sear for 20 seconds on each side. Transfer the slices onto a serving platter, slightly overlapping them. Repeat with the remaining salmon.

ASSEMBLY Sprinkle jalapeño slices over each piece of salmon. Spoon ponzu sauce over the salmon and serve immediately.

GOOD TO KNOW When shopping for fresh fish, it pays to be picky. Here are a few ways to check for freshness:

Fish should have a mild scent and smell salty and of the sea. Stay away from anything that has a strong, fishy odor.

The eyes should be clear, bright, and bulging, not cloudy.

Fish should be shiny and remain firm when you poke it with your finger, not slimy to touch.

GOOD TO KNOW Salmon should be sliced and seared no more than 1 hour before serving.

GOOD TO KNOW Ponzu Sauce should be spooned over the salmon just before serving.

MAKE IT AHEAD Ponzu Sauce can be prepared in advance and stored in the refrigerator for up to 4 days.

Crudo, Italy's take on raw fish, is often thinly sliced and dressed with citrus and olive oil. The key is to prepare food with fine ingredients, so you don't need to do much else to it. In this case, a fresh, high-quality fish amplified with thinly sliced radishes, a little salt and pepper, citrus, and olive oil yields remarkable results.

TUNA CRUDO WITH RADISH, CITRUS ZEST, AND SHALLOT

READY IN 15 MINUTES

SERVES 8

2 (8-oz) sushi-grade tuna loin steaks

½ tsp kosher salt

Freshly ground black pepper

5 radishes, thinly sliced

1 shallot, thinly sliced

Grated zest and juice of 1 orange (about ¼ cup)

Grated zest and juice of 1 lime (about 2 Tbsp)

3 Tbsp extra-virgin olive oil

Using a chef's knife, slice the tuna across the grain into ¼-inch-thick slices. Season with salt and pepper, then place on a serving platter. Arrange radishes, scatter shallot, and sprinkle the citrus zest on top.

In a small bowl, whisk together the orange and lime juices and olive oil. Spoon the oil over the tuna and serve immediately.

GOOD TO KNOW Tuna Crudo should be sliced no more than 1 hour before serving.

GOOD TO KNOW Tuna Crudo should be dressed just before serving. If citrus juice is added too early, the fish will "cook" from the acidity in the citrus.

GET ORGANIZED For uniform crudo slices, place the tuna in the freezer for 10 minutes before slicing.

SUBSTITUTIONS Tuna Crudo can be made with sushi-grade salmon as well.

A crisp skin adds a layer of texture to this soft, flaky salmon dish. I highly recommend reading the recipe in its entirety (along with the tips) before starting to familiarize yourself with the technique. It's certainly not difficult, but advanced knowledge of the recipe will keep you prepared and organized. This dish is most delicious as soon as it comes off the pan, so I often save this recipe for more intimate meals with two to four people.

CRISPY-SKINNED SALMON

READY IN 20 MINUTES

SERVES 4

4 (8-oz) salmon fillets, skin on

2 tsp neutral oil such as avocado oil, vegetable oil, or rice bran oil (divided)

Kosher salt and coarsely ground black pepper

1 lemon, thinly sliced, for garnish

Fresh chopped herbs, for garnish

SPECIAL TOOLS OR EQUIPMENT

Stainless-steel fish spatula

GOOD TO KNOW Do *not* use a nonstick pan! Using an uncoated pan results in crispier salmon skin.

GOOD TO KNOW Season the salmon with salt just before searing. Salting the skin too early results in the skin releasing moisture and not crisping up while cooking.

GOOD TO KNOW Determine your preferred level of doneness by gauging the color of the salmon's sides: bright pink for medium-rare; light pink for medium; and pale pink for well done.

Rinse the salmon fillets under cold running water and pat dry using paper towels.

Heat a large uncoated pan (see tip below) over medium-high heat. Once you feel heat emitting from the pan, dab the salmon skin once more with paper towels.

Add 1 teaspoon of oil to coat the bottom of the pan. The pan should shimmer but not smoke. (If the pan is smoking, remove it from the heat for 1 minute and reduce the heat slightly.) Generously season both sides of 2 fillets with salt and pepper and place into the pan, skin-side down. (They will sizzle.) Press down on the fillets with a stainless-steel fish spatula and fry for 7 minutes, until the skin is golden brown and crisp. (You can use the spatula to lift the fillets slightly to check.) Carefully flip the fillets and cook for another 30 seconds. It's worth noting that about 90% of the cooking will take place when the salmon fillets are skin-side down and you are pressing down on them. When you flip the fillets, you are cooking for another 30 seconds just to get a hint of sear.

Transfer the fillets, skin-side up, onto a serving plate. Add another teaspoon of oil to the pan and repeat with the remaining fillets.

Garnish with lemon slices and chopped herbs and serve immediately.

Don't get me started—when it comes to smoked salmon, I am a major snob!
I am incredibly particular, and I like mine super-thinly sliced. And, when I serve
it in my house, I give it the respect it deserves. This is how smoked salmon is
meant to be eaten.

SMOKED SALMON WITH SHALLOT, DILL, AND LEMON

READY IN 10 MINUTES

SERVES 8

2 lbs smoked Nova Scotia salmon, thinly sliced

1 lemon, thinly sliced and pips removed

1 shallot, thinly sliced

2 Tbsp finely chopped dill

Pinch of kosher salt

¼ tsp freshly ground black pepper

¼ cup extra-virgin olive oil

Bagels, to serve

Capers, to serve

Sliced tomatoes, to serve

Sliced radishes, to serve

Place the smoked salmon in a single layer on a large platter, with pieces slightly overlapping. Arrange lemon slices, shallot, and dill on top. Season with salt and pepper. Drizzle with olive oil and serve immediately with bagels, capers, tomatoes, and radishes.

MAKE IT AHEAD The smoked salmon can be garnished with shallot and dill and stored in the refrigerator for up to 3 hours. Add the lemon, salt, pepper, and oil just before serving.

This is my kosher take on crab cakes. Chopping fresh salmon in a food processor is an easy way to give this fish a whole new look and taste, and sesame and scallion pair up beautifully to enhance taste. I like to quickly pan-fry them in hot oil, then finish them off in the oven. The result? A deliciously moist salmon cake with a crisp exterior that makes for a light and satisfying lunch.

SESAME-SCALLION SALMON CAKES

READY IN 25–30 MINUTES

SERVES 6

2 lbs salmon fillets, skin removed

1 bunch scallions, trimmed and roughly chopped

1 Tbsp mayonnaise

1 tsp Dijon mustard

2 Tbsp black or white sesame seeds

1 tsp kosher salt

½ tsp freshly ground black pepper

½ tsp garlic powder

3 Tbsp neutral oil such as avocado oil, vegetable oil, or rice bran oil

Lightly dressed leafy salad, to serve

SPECIAL TOOLS OR EQUIPMENT
Food processor

Preheat oven to 400°F. Line a baking sheet with parchment paper.

Place salmon in a food processor fitted with the metal blade and process until finely chopped. Add scallions and process for another minute, until well mixed.

Transfer the salmon mixture to a medium bowl. Add mayonnaise, mustard, sesame seeds, salt, pepper, and garlic powder. Using your hands, mix well.

With damp hands, form 3 tablespoons of mixture into a ball. Press down gently to form a patty. Transfer to the prepared baking sheet. Repeat until all of the mixture is used.

Heat oil in a large nonstick skillet over medium-high heat. Working in batches to avoid overcrowding, add the salmon cakes and pan-fry for 1–2 minutes per side, until golden. Transfer the salmon cakes back to the baking sheet. Repeat with the remaining cakes.

Once all the salmon cakes are seared, bake them for 5–7 minutes, until plump, sizzling, and cooked through. (No need to flip over.)

Transfer to a serving platter and serve immediately with a side of salad.

GOOD TO KNOW "Overcrowding the pan" refers to adding too many ingredients to a pan at once. When the pan is overcrowded, too much steam is created, and instead of the food frying or searing, it steam-cooks and turns soggy.

MAKE IT AHEAD The Sesame-Scallion Salmon Cakes mixture may be frozen. Form the salmon cakes into patties and place them on a parchment-lined baking sheet. Place the baking sheet in the freezer for 1–2 hours, until the patties are frozen.

Transfer the salmon cakes to a freezer bag and store them in the freezer for up to 1 month. When ready to serve, simply thaw and cook as per instructions.

I'm a huge fan of Teri Turner, the creator of @nocrumbsleft, and I am inspired by everything that she cooks—her style is so straightforward. She revolutionized the sliced onion when the "marinated onion recipe" from her cookbook *No Crumbs Left* received a TON of buzz. I was hooked—and I still am. This is one of the ways I use Teri's magical onions.

GRILLED HALIBUT WITH MARINATED ONIONS

READY IN 25 MINUTES

SERVES 6

MARINATED ONIONS

1 small red onion, very thinly sliced

½ cup extra-virgin olive oil

1 Tbsp red wine vinegar

1 tsp dried oregano

½ tsp kosher salt

¼ tsp freshly ground black pepper

HALIBUT

6 (10-oz) halibut steaks

½ tsp kosher salt

¼ tsp freshly ground black pepper

Grated zest and juice of 1 lemon (about 3 Tbsp)

1 Tbsp extra-virgin olive oil

2 Tbsp finely chopped flat-leaf parsley

SPECIAL TOOLS OR EQUIPMENT

Outdoor grill or indoor grill pan

MARINATED ONIONS In a medium bowl, combine all ingredients and toss well. Set aside to marinate for at least 10 minutes or up to 1 week (see tip below).

HALIBUT Preheat an outdoor grill or indoor grill pan over medium-high heat.

Season halibut with salt and pepper.

In a small bowl, whisk together lemon zest and juice, olive oil, and parsley.

Pour the sauce over the halibut and marinate for 5 minutes.

Brush the grill with some of the marinade to prevent the halibut from sticking. Place halibut on the grill and grill for 5 minutes on each side, until firm to the touch.

Transfer to a serving platter and top with a mound of marinated onions. Serve immediately.

MAKE IT AHEAD The onions can be marinated at room temperature for up to 12 hours. After that, marinate them for up to 1 week in the refrigerator. If refrigerated, set onions aside at room temperature before serving (this allows the oil to liquify).

Don't think twice about preparing and cooking whole fish at home. It's nearly impossible to mess up. Start with good-quality fresh fish and have your fishmonger gut and debone the fish for you. Here, I've prepared the whole branzino with a classic aromatic blend of lemon, thyme, and garlic—a simple reminder that you only need a few fresh ingredients to create a gourmet meal.

BRANZINO WITH LEMON, THYME, AND GARLIC

READY IN 30 MINUTES

SERVES 6

6 (1-lb) branzinos, scaled, gutted, deboned, and heads and tails removed

Kosher salt and freshly ground black pepper

3 cloves garlic, thinly sliced

2 lemons, sliced into thin rounds and pips removed

12 sprigs thyme

Extra-virgin olive oil, for drizzling

SPECIAL TOOLS OR EQUIPMENT

Outdoor grill or indoor grill pan

Preheat an outdoor grill or indoor grill pan over medium-high heat. Line a baking sheet with parchment paper.

Rinse branzinos under cold water and pat dry with paper towels. Transfer branzinos onto the prepared baking sheet. Generously season the outside and inside cavities with salt and pepper. Place 3–4 garlic slices, 4 lemon slices, and 2 sprigs of thyme into the cavity of each branzino.

Drizzle 1–2 teaspoons of olive oil over each fish. Using your hands, rub the oil into the skin of the fish.

Transfer branzinos from baking sheet to grill or pan. Grill for 7 minutes on each side, until firm to the touch.

Transfer to a platter and serve immediately.

SUBSTITUTIONS Don't have an outdoor grill or indoor grill pan? No worries! Whole branzino can also be roasted in the oven. Preheat oven to 450°F and roast branzino on a parchment-lined baking sheet for 8–10 minutes. Turn over and roast for another 8–10 minutes, until firm to the touch and crisp on the outside.

There's so much versatility with this easy recipe. Grab any herbs in your refrigerator (even if they're wilted), add a handful of breadcrumbs or crackers (or potato chips!), and blitz them together for a delicious and golden herb-crumb fish topping. It's that simple.

15-MINUTE HERB-CRUMBED FISH

READY IN 15 MINUTES

SERVES 6

6 (8-oz) fillets of fish of your choice

Kosher salt and freshly ground black pepper

Handful of fresh herbs such as dill, parsley, basil, or cilantro, leaves only

Juice of ½ lemon (about 1½ Tbsp)

1 tsp yellow mustard

¼ cup breadcrumbs or a handful of crackers (such as Ritz or saltines)

1 tsp extra-virgin olive oil, for drizzling

Lightly dressed salad, to serve

SPECIAL TOOLS OR EQUIPMENT
Food processor or blender

Preheat oven to 425°F. Line a baking sheet with parchment paper.

Place fillets on the prepared baking sheet and season with salt and pepper.

In a food processor or blender, combine herbs, lemon juice, and mustard and blitz until chopped finely. Stir in breadcrumbs (or crackers). Season with salt and pepper.

Sprinkle the crumb mixture over the fish fillets. Bake, uncovered, for 12 minutes, until cooked through.

Drizzle olive oil over the fillets and serve immediately with a side of salad.

GOOD TO KNOW Herb crumbs are a great way to use up near-expired herbs.

MAKE IT AHEAD The herb crumb can be prepared in advance and stored in the refrigerator for up to 3 days or in the freezer for 1 month. I always have a bag of herb crumbs stored in the freezer, perfect for super-quick dinners.

This is my "go-to" recipe for pleasing everyone at home with just one dish (I wish that would happen more often!), and I usually serve it with french fries as a take on "fish-and-chips." I've omitted the traditional relish or pickle ingredient in the tartar sauce because it's not my thing; however, add some if you feel inclined. And a little hot sauce never hurt anyone.

FRIED GREY SOLE WITH LEMON AND TARTAR SAUCE

READY IN 30 MINUTES

SERVES 6

TARTAR SAUCE

¾ cup mayonnaise

1 Tbsp grainy Dijon

½ tsp Worcestershire sauce

Juice of ½ lemon (about 1 ½ Tbsp)

2 Tbsp finely chopped dill

1 Tbsp chopped capers

Kosher salt and freshly ground black pepper

GREY SOLE

6 (6–8-oz) grey sole fillets

Kosher salt and freshly ground black pepper

2 eggs

1 Tbsp water

2 cups seasoned breadcrumbs (I like the Israeli-style breadcrumbs with sesame seeds)

½ cup neutral oil such as avocado oil, vegetable oil, or rice bran oil

2 lemons, cut into wedges

SPECIAL TOOLS OR EQUIPMENT

Stainless-steel fish spatula

TARTAR SAUCE In a small bowl, combine all ingredients and mix well. Season with salt and pepper. Cover and store in the refrigerator until ready to serve.

GREY SOLE Line a baking sheet with parchment paper. Season fish fillets with salt and pepper.

In a shallow bowl, combine eggs and water and whisk well.

Pour breadcrumbs into a large shallow dish.

Working with 1 fillet at a time, dip the fillet into the egg and then coat completely in breadcrumbs. Place the coated fillet onto the prepared baking sheet. Repeat with the remaining fillets.

Heat oil in a large nonstick skillet over medium-high heat. Test the heat of the oil by sprinkling a few breadcrumbs into the pan—if it sizzles, the oil is ready.

Working in batches to avoid overcrowding, place 1–2 fillets in the pan and fry for 3 minutes, until golden. Using a stainless-steel fish spatula, carefully flip the fillet(s) and fry for another 2 minutes. Transfer fish to paper towel–lined plate to drain. Repeat with the remaining fillets.

Transfer fillets to a platter, then add lemon wedges. Serve immediately with tartar sauce.

GOOD TO KNOW Most fried foods will continue to cook for a few minutes and even darken in color after they are removed from the pan or oven.

MAKE IT AHEAD Tartar Sauce can be made up to 2 days in advance and stored in the refrigerator.

Turmeric is a potent anti-inflammatory and antioxidant that has been scientifically proven to prevent heart disease. I laud it for its remarkable health benefits, but I also love the way it adds a shocking goldenrod color to my cooking. This dish is full of vibrant color, surprisingly delicate in flavor, and simply delicious.

SEA BASS WITH TURMERIC, CARROT, AND CHICKPEAS

READY IN 35 MINUTES

SERVES 6

2 Tbsp light olive oil

1 small yellow onion, thinly sliced

2 cloves garlic, minced

1 tsp ground turmeric

5 carrots, cut into thin, long ribbons

2 (15 ½-oz) cans chickpeas, drained

1 jalapeño (optional)

Juice of ½ lemon (about 1 ½ Tbsp)

Kosher salt and freshly ground black pepper

6 (8-oz) skinless sea bass fillets

Handful of flat-leaf parsley, roughly chopped

Heat olive oil in a large nonstick skillet over medium-high heat. Add onion and sauté for 5–7 minutes, until softened and translucent. Add garlic and stir in turmeric. Cook for 2 minutes.

Add carrots, chickpeas, whole jalapeño, if using, and lemon juice and gently mix. Reduce heat to medium and sauté for 5 minutes, or until carrots are slightly softened. Season with salt and pepper. Using a wooden spoon, move the chickpea mixture to the sides of the pan.

Season the sea bass with a little salt and pepper. (You don't want to over-season here since the chickpea mixture is already seasoned.) Add all of the sea bass to the center of the pan and spoon the chickpea mixture over the fish.

Increase the temperature to medium-high heat until mixture comes to a boil. Then reduce to medium-low heat, cover, and cook for 12–15 minutes, until fish is cooked through.

Transfer to a serving platter. Garnish with parsley and serve immediately.

SUBSTITUTIONS The parsley can be replaced with any fresh chopped herbs.

MAKE IT AHEAD The chickpea mixture can be prepared in advance and stored in the refrigerator for up to 3 days. When you're ready to prepare the fish, transfer the chickpea mixture to a nonstick skillet, add the sea bass, and cook as instructed in the recipe.

Bright, coral-fleshed Arctic char is a mild fish in the salmon family. I serve a whole side of the char family-style with a crunchy, spicy, and zesty topping. Paired with a loaf of crusty sourdough and a couple bottles of red, you don't need much else.

ARCTIC CHAR WITH CHILI, HAZELNUT, AND DILL OIL

READY IN 30 MINUTES

SERVES 6

Cooking spray

1 (2-lb) side of Arctic char, skin on and pin bones removed

Kosher salt and freshly ground black pepper

3 Tbsp roughly chopped roasted and skinned hazelnuts

1–2 Tbsp roughly chopped dill

Grated zest of ½ orange

¼ cup extra-virgin olive oil

¼ tsp chili flakes

Preheat oven to 425°F. Grease a baking sheet with cooking spray.

Place the char on the prepared baking sheet and season with salt and pepper. Bake for 18–20 minutes, until opaque.

Meanwhile, in a small bowl, combine hazelnuts, dill, orange zest, olive oil, and chili flakes. Season generously with salt and pepper and mix well.

When the char is ready, spoon the sauce over the fish and serve immediately.

MAKE IT AHEAD Arctic char can be cooked up to 3 hours ahead of time and left on the counter until you're ready to serve. Serve at room temperature.

MAKE IT AHEAD The chili, hazelnut, and dill oil can be prepared up to 3 days in advance and stored in a glass jar in the refrigerator until ready to serve.

GOURMET GIFTS

Over the years, I've come to realize that a homemade gift can go a long way. A personal gift often strikes a chord in people, and I'm always taken aback by the reactions. In fact, I enjoy it almost as much as I love cooking… *almost*.

Here are some of my go-to gourmet gifts. When it comes to making a lasting impression, the presentation is equally important. There are many beautiful, simple, and memorable ways of wrapping your homemade presents with ribbon, twine, and cellophane or packing them into paper lunch bags.

Each of these recipes makes enough for four homemade gifts. Feel free to adjust accordingly for your guest list.

NUT AND HONEY JARS

Assorted roasted whole nuts
(almonds, pecans, cashews)

Aromatics such as cinnamon sticks, star anise,
vanilla bean, dried fig, or small dried chile

4 slices of orange peel

High-quality honey

4 (5-oz) wide-mouth glass jars

Decorative ribbons

4 wooden honey dippers or cinnamon sticks

Fill each jar halfway with nuts, then add
aromatics and orange peel. Pour in enough
honey to fill each jar. Wrap ribbon around each
and tuck in the honey dipper or cinnamon stick.
Serve as a topping. Nut and honey jars can be
stored in a pantry for up to 3 months.

FLAVORED VODKA

Pomegranate seeds

4–8 sprigs sage

Your favorite vodka

4 (8-oz) apothecary glass bottles or glass milk bottles

Kitchen twine

Paper tags

Add pomegranate seeds and sage to each
bottle. Pour in vodka, seal bottle, and give it a
quick shake. Thread twine through the paper
tags, then wrap one around the neck of each
bottle. Vodka should "steep" for 1 week. When
ready to enjoy, simply chill, strain, and serve.
Flavored vodkas can be stored in the freezer
for up to 1 month.

GARLIC CONFIT

2 cups peeled garlic cloves

Extra-virgin olive oil, to cover

2 lemons, rinsed, very thinly sliced
and pips removed

Sprig of thyme

4 (4-oz) glass jars with tight-fitting lid or clamp lid

Preheat oven to 350°F. Place garlic in a small shallow baking dish. Pour olive oil over top, then add lemon and thyme. Bake, uncovered, for 30 minutes, until garlic is softened and light brown. Cool completely, then distribute evenly among clean glass jars. Garlic confit can be added to stews or used as a condiment or a dipping sauce. It can be stored in the refrigerator for up to 1 month. Bring to room temperature to liquify oil before use.

QUICK PRESERVED LEMON

12 lemons, rinsed and thinly sliced

4 tsp kosher salt

1 tsp chili flakes (optional)

Extra-virgin olive oil

4 (2-oz) glass jars with tight-fitting lid or clamp lid

In a large bowl, combine lemons, salt, and chili flakes, if using, and mix well. Distribute lemons among the glass jars until jars are completely packed, then drizzle a little olive oil over top. Seal tightly. Store in a cool place for 1 week. Rinse preserved lemon slices before using. Preserved lemons can be stored in the refrigerator for up to 2 months.

MEAT AND POULTRY

Learn to take risks and have the courage to change things around or make a recipe work even if you don't have every single ingredient.

STYLING TIP

No table setting is cleaner and crisper than simple white dishes on white table linen. This classic look never goes wrong and continues to be my go-to table setting time after time.

"Confit" comes from the French word *confire*, meaning "to preserve." Slow-cooking garlic in oil creates a rich yet mellow flavor. For this recipe, you'll need to first prepare the garlic confit with lemon and thyme, and then add the chicken to cook in the confit.

Garlic confit can be used as a condiment, so I always keep a jar of it in my refrigerator. Once you have the garlic confit on hand, you can have a delicious meal on the table in a fraction of the time.

GARLIC-CONFIT CHICKEN WITH LEMON AND THYME

READY IN 1 HOUR AND 50 MINUTES

SERVES 4–6

20 cloves garlic, peeled

1 lemon, very thinly sliced and pips removed

5–6 sprigs thyme

½ cup extra-virgin olive oil

1 (3-lb) whole chicken, cut into 8 pieces, skin on and bone in, trimmed of excess skin and fat

Kosher salt and freshly ground black pepper

2 Tbsp balsamic vinegar

2 tsp honey

Preheat oven to 325°F.

Combine garlic, lemon, and thyme into a baking dish that is large enough to hold the chicken. Pour in olive oil and bake, uncovered, for 35 minutes, until garlic has softened. Set aside for 10 minutes to cool slightly. Increase the oven temperature to 375°F.

Generously season chicken with salt and pepper. Using your hands, rub vinegar and honey over the chicken.

Using a wooden spoon, move the garlic mixture to the sides of the baking dish to create a space in the center. Add the chicken to the center of the dish and spoon the garlic mixture on top of the chicken.

Cover with an ovenproof lid or aluminum foil. Bake for 40 minutes. Uncover the dish and bake for another 20 minutes, until the chicken is cooked through.

Discard thyme sprigs and serve.

SUBSTITUTIONS You can experiment with different herbs.

OMISSIONS Prepare garlic confit with or without the lemon and thyme.

MAKE IT AHEAD Garlic confit with lemon and thyme can be prepared, cooled, and stored in a glass jar with a tight-fitting lid for up to 2 weeks in the refrigerator. Before use, bring to room temperature to liquify the oil.

REHEAT Garlic-Confit Chicken can be reheated, uncovered, in a 350°F oven for about 10 minutes.

GARLIC-CONFIT CHICKEN WITH LEMON AND THYME

Juicy, flavorful, and, above all, uncomplicated—now this is how to cook chicken! The key to this recipe is the herbaceous paste made with fresh chopped herbs, lemon juice, olive oil, and mayonnaise. While mayo might seem unusual, it serves to crisp up the skin and keep the meat moist and delectable.

CRISPY CHICKEN WITH HERBS AND WHITE WINE

READY IN 1 HOUR AND 20 MINUTES

SERVES 8

1 (3-lb) whole chicken, butterflied

Kosher salt and freshly ground black pepper

1 head garlic, unpeeled

¼ cup extra-virgin olive oil (divided)

2 Tbsp finely chopped flat-leaf parsley

1 Tbsp finely chopped rosemary

1 Tbsp finely chopped thyme

¼ cup mayonnaise

1 cup dry white wine, chicken stock, or vegetable stock

GOOD TO KNOW Covering the chicken with aluminum foil and allowing it to rest for 5–10 minutes after it's cooked helps to recirculate the juices throughout the meat, resulting in a juicier, tastier chicken.

MAKE IT AHEAD The herb paste can be prepared and stored in the refrigerator up to 3 days in advance.

MAKE IT AHEAD This recipe can be assembled and marinated and stored in the refrigerator for up to 24 hours. Bring to room temperature before cooking.

Preheat oven to 450°F.

Season the inside and outside of the chicken generously with salt and pepper. Place chicken, breast-side up, into a large cast-iron skillet or ovenproof pan.

Cut the garlic head crosswise to expose the individual cloves. Drizzle 1 ½ teaspoons of olive oil over the exposed cloves, then season with salt and pepper. Tuck the garlic halves under the chicken.

In a small bowl, combine herbs, mayonnaise, and 3½ tablespoons of olive oil and mix well to form a paste. Using your hands, rub the paste all over the chicken and carefully under the skin.

Pour wine (or stock) into the pan, but not directly over the chicken. Cover with an ovenproof lid or aluminum foil. Roast for 30 minutes.

Uncover, baste, and roast for another 20–30 minutes.

Remove the pan from the oven and cover tightly. Set aside the chicken to rest for 5–10 minutes. To serve, remove the garlic halves under the chicken and serve them alongside.

REHEAT Chicken can be reheated, covered, in a 350°F oven for about 10 minutes.

I am always on the hunt for easy and inspired chicken recipes, and I'm pleased to share this one with you. Juicy strips of marinated chicken, tender artichoke hearts, and sweet caramelized fennel come together in this expressive Mediterranean dish.

CHICKEN WITH ARTICHOKES AND FENNEL

READY IN 1 HOUR

SERVES 6

6 skinless and boneless chicken breasts, pounded and cut into 1-inch strips

Kosher salt and freshly ground black pepper

3 Tbsp extra-virgin olive oil, plus extra for greasing

1 yellow onion, thinly sliced

1 fennel bulb, trimmed, thick outer layers removed, and thinly sliced

1 (10-oz) bag frozen artichoke hearts, quartered

2 cloves garlic, minced

1 Tbsp dried rosemary

2 Tbsp balsamic vinegar

1 Tbsp grainy Dijon

Juice of 1 lemon (about 3 Tbsp)

Microgreens, for garnish (optional)

SPECIAL TOOLS OR EQUIPMENT
Indoor grill pan (optional)

Place chicken in a baking dish. Season generously on both sides with salt and pepper. In a large mixing bowl, combine all remaining ingredients except microgreens and mix well. Pour mixture over chicken, cover, and marinate for at least 30 minutes or up to 24 hours. If marinating for longer than 30 minutes, place the baking dish in the refrigerator.

Heat an indoor grill pan or nonstick skillet over high heat. Lightly grease the pan with olive oil to prevent sticking. Transfer the marinated ingredients into the pan, give it a good shake, and sauté for 5 minutes. Reduce the heat to medium. Cover and cook for 7 minutes.

Uncover and cook for another 7 minutes, rotating the ingredients occasionally, until the chicken is cooked through and the vegetables are caramelized.

Transfer to a serving platter and garnish with microgreens, if using.

SUBSTITUTIONS The yellow onion can be replaced with any onion variety.

SUBSTITUTIONS If you can only find whole artichokes, lightly thaw and quarter.

MAKE IT AHEAD Chicken with Artichokes and Fennel can be assembled and marinated in advance and stored in the refrigerator for up to 24 hours. Bring to room temperature before cooking.

REHEAT Bring Chicken with Artichokes and Fennel to room temperature, cover, and reheat in a 350°F oven for about 10 minutes.

This recipe reminds us that you don't need expensive cuts of meat to produce an elegant entrée. As always, start with high-quality seasonal ingredients to ensure the best results. Here, fresh figs transform the expected into something truly exceptional.

CHICKEN WITH RED ONION AND FIG SAUCE

READY IN 1 HOUR

SERVES 6

1 Tbsp light olive oil, plus extra for greasing

1 red onion, thinly sliced

4 black or green figs, stemmed and quartered

Grated zest of 1 orange

½ cup ketchup

¼ cup water

2 Tbsp balsamic vinegar

1 Tbsp honey

Kosher salt and freshly ground black pepper

10 chicken thighs, skin on and bone-in, patted dry

Handful of basil, finely chopped

Preheat oven to 375°F. Lightly grease a baking dish large enough to hold chicken.

Heat olive oil in a large nonstick skillet over medium-high heat. Add onion and sauté for 5 minutes, until translucent and slightly browned.

Add figs, orange zest, ketchup, water, vinegar, and honey and stir well. Bring to a boil, then reduce heat to low. Simmer for 5 minutes, stirring constantly. Season with salt and pepper. Remove from the heat and set aside to cool slightly.

Season chicken with salt and pepper. Transfer chicken to the prepared baking dish. Pour the sauce over top and shake the baking dish to coat chicken. Cover the dish with aluminum foil and bake for 30 minutes. Uncover, then cook for another 10 minutes, until cooked through.

Remove foil, scatter basil on top, and serve.

SUBSTITUTIONS Red Onion and Fig Sauce can be made with dried figs, if fresh ones are unavailable. Soak 5 dried figs in boiling water for 2 minutes, then quarter them and use as instructed in the recipe.

MAKE IT AHEAD Red Onion and Fig Sauce can be prepared in advance and stored in the refrigerator for up to 5 days. The sauce should be brought to room temperature before it's poured over the chicken.

MAKE IT AHEAD Chicken with Red Onion and Fig Sauce can be assembled and marinated in advance and refrigerated for up to 24 hours. Bring it to room temperature before cooking.

REHEAT Leftovers can be covered and reheated in a 350°F oven for about 10 minutes.

If you have about an hour to whip up dinner, I recommend this all-in-one dish with flavorful pesto-rubbed chicken, tender golden potatoes, and crisp red onions. Store-bought pesto makes this recipe super simple, and a touch of fresh lemon zest lifts and brightens up the dish. Dinner is served.

LEMON-PESTO CHICKEN WITH POTATOES AND RED ONIONS

READY IN 1 HOUR AND 20 MINUTES

SERVES 4–6

1 (3-lb) whole chicken, cut into 8 pieces, skin on and bone-in, trimmed of excess skin and fat

Kosher salt and freshly ground black pepper

5 Yukon gold potatoes, cut into ¼-inch cubes

1 red onion, thinly sliced

Grated zest of 1 lemon

1 cup store-bought or prepared pesto

1 tsp dried basil

Preheat oven to 375°F.

Place chicken in a large baking dish and generously season all sides with salt and pepper. Add potatoes, onion, lemon zest, pesto, and basil, and season with a little more salt and pepper. Using your hands, rub the pesto over the chicken, potatoes, and onions.

Cover with aluminum foil and bake for 45 minutes. Uncover and cook for another 20 minutes, until crisp and golden.

MAKE IT AHEAD Lemon-Pesto Chicken with Potatoes and Red Onions can be assembled and marinated in the refrigerator for up to 24 hours. Bring to room temperature before cooking.

STORAGE Lemon-Pesto Chicken with Potatoes and Red Onions can be reheated, uncovered, in a 350°F oven for about 10 minutes.

Bibimbap, which translates in Korean to "mixed rice with meat and assorted vegetables," is always a bowl of comfort. Steamed rice is topped with various proteins, a fried egg, and sharp pickled vegetables. Sometimes all I need to do is to serve an unusually named recipe, and everything else falls into place.

BIBIMBAP

2 cups white or brown rice

2 Tbsp neutral oil such as avocado oil, vegetable oil, or rice bran oil (divided)

1 clove garlic, minced

1 (10-oz) package frozen chopped spinach, thawed and squeezed of excess moisture

Kosher salt and freshly ground black pepper

6 eggs

2–3 cups leftover chicken, beef, lamb, fish, or veggies, slightly heated

1 Tbsp black sesame seeds

1 cup Quick Pickled Vegetable Chips (p. 46)

Hot sauce or Sriracha (optional)

Cook rice according to package directions. Keep warm and set aside.

Heat 1 tablespoon of oil in a nonstick skillet over medium-high heat. Add garlic and cook for 1 minute, until fragrant. Add spinach and cook for 5 minutes. Season generously with salt and pepper.

Transfer spinach to a small bowl, then cover with aluminum foil to keep warm.

Return the skillet to medium-high heat. Add the remaining 1 table-spoon of oil to the skillet. Crack the eggs, one at a time, first into a small bowl and then gently into the hot oil. Fry for 5 minutes.

Scoop ½ cup of rice into 6 individual serving bowls, and top with a handful of warm leftover chicken, meat, fish, or veggies. Add a heaping tablespoon of sautéed spinach, then sprinkle sesame seeds on top. Add 2–3 tablespoons of pickled vegetable chips to the bowl. Gently top each bowl with a fried egg. Drizzle hot sauce (or Sriracha) on top, if using.

Classic kosher turkey is easy to make, but there are no shortcuts. I encourage you to read through the entire recipe, including the tips, to familiarize yourself with the process before you start. I assure you that all of the attention will pay off, and you'll be serving up golden, crispy turkey (on both sides, not just the top!) full of juicy flavor with a rich, velvety gravy to boot.

CLASSIC KOSHER TURKEY

READY IN 4 HOURS (IT'S WORTH IT)

SERVES 8–12

GARLIC-HERB "BUTTER"

3 heads garlic

3 Tbsp extra-virgin olive oil (divided)

Kosher salt

1 bunch flat-leaf parsley

10 sage leaves

1 Tbsp thyme leaves

Freshly ground black pepper

GARLIC-HERB "BUTTER" Preheat oven to 350°F.

Slice off the top of each garlic head to reveal the cloves. Place the heads together on a large piece of aluminum foil. Drizzle with 1 tablespoon olive oil and a pinch of salt. Wrap completely in the foil, place in a baking dish, and bake for 40 minutes, until garlic has softened. Remove from the oven and set aside for 5 minutes. Increase the oven temperature to 375°F.

Squeeze the base of the garlic heads to release the softened garlic cloves. Discard the skins and the heads.

Transfer cloves to a food processor or a blender. Add parsley, sage, thyme, and the remaining 2 tablespoons of olive oil. Process until smooth and creamy. Season generously with salt and pepper. Set aside.

TIPS FOR SUCCESS

The perfect kosher turkey requires a degree of patience, but all that hard work will pay off. (Maybe it's a good thing that Thanksgiving only comes around once a year!) Here are a few tips to ensure optimal results.

A frozen turkey can take up to 4 days to defrost in the refrigerator. Please factor in the defrost time when preparing your turkey.

Garlic-Herb "Butter" can be prepared in advance and stored in the refrigerator for up to 4 days.

The turkey can be cleaned, trimmed, tied up, and stored in the refrigerator up to 2 days in advance until ready to prepare and cook.

The turkey can be rubbed with Garlic-Herb "Butter," the cavity can be stuffed, and the onions, carrots, and celery can be scattered in the roasting pan and stored in the refrigerator up to 2 days in advance.

Any herb of your choice can be used for Garlic-Herb "Butter" and to stuff the cavity.

Leaving the peel on your onion results in a beautiful, golden-colored gravy.

Placing a rack in the roasting pan keeps the turkey slightly raised in the pan, preventing it from sitting in the liquid and resulting in an evenly cooked and crispy turkey. Additionally, since the turkey is raised, the drippings collect in the liquid below and result in a flavorful gravy.

1 (12–14-lb) kosher turkey, cleaned, trimmed, and patted dry

Kosher salt and freshly ground black pepper

1 lemon, cut in half

6 sprigs thyme

3 yellow onions, unpeeled and quartered (divided)

1 qty Garlic-Herb "Butter" (see here)

4 carrots

3 celery stalks and leaves

1 cup white wine

1 cup turkey, chicken, or vegetable stock

2 Tbsp mayonnaise

1 tsp paprika

½ tsp ground turmeric

1 tsp all-purpose flour (optional)

SPECIAL TOOLS OR EQUIPMENT

Electric knife or chef's knife

Food processor or blender

Instant-read meat thermometer

Kitchen twine

Large roasting pan

Pastry brush

Rimmed cutting board

Roasting rack

Turkey baster

TURKEY Trim away any excess skin or fat from the turkey. Lay the turkey on the counter, breast-side up. Cross the legs one over the other and use kitchen twine to tie the narrowest part of the legs together.

Season the outside of the turkey and the cavity generously with salt and pepper. Stuff the cavity with lemon, thyme, and 4 onion quarters.

Using your hands, rub Garlic-Herb "Butter" all over the turkey. Gently pull up the turkey skin and rub more herb "butter" under the skin and into the meat. Rub the remaining herb "butter" over the sides of the turkey.

Place the turkey on a rack (see tip on previous page) in a large roasting pan, breast-side up.

Scatter remaining onion quarters, carrots, and celery in the pan, around the turkey. Pour wine and stock over the onions, carrots, and celery (but not over the turkey).

In a small bowl, combine mayonnaise, paprika, and turmeric.

Gently pat the turkey skin with a paper towel to remove any excess moisture. Do not wipe off the herb "butter," just gently pat the top. Brush the top of the turkey with the mayonnaise mixture. Loosely cover the turkey with aluminum foil and roast for 1 hour.

Remove the foil. Using a turkey baster, baste the turkey with the liquid in the pan. Roast the turkey, uncovered, for another 45 minutes.

Remove the turkey from the oven and carefully flip it over (see tip) so that the bottom side is exposed. Baste the turkey and roast, uncovered, for an additional 30–45 minutes, until the skin is golden brown.

Remove the turkey from the oven and flip it over again, so it is breast-side up. Baste again and roast, uncovered, for another 1 hour, until the turkey is golden brown, glistening, and plump.

Remove the turkey from the oven. Carefully transfer the turkey from the roasting pan to a rimmed cutting board. Cover the turkey with foil and set aside to rest for 1 hour.

Discard the onion, carrots, celery, and herbs. Ladle the roasting liquid through a fine-mesh sieve into a large saucepan. This will be the basis of your gravy.

Place the pan on the stovetop and simmer over medium-high heat for 8–10 minutes, stirring continuously, until thickened. For a thicker sauce, whisk in flour. Generously season with salt and pepper. Reduce temperature to medium-low and keep warm until serving.

Using a chef's knife or an electric knife, carve the turkey and serve with gravy.

TIPS FOR SUCCESS

Turkey cooking time per weight: Typically, a turkey cooks for 13 minutes per pound. So, the time required to cook a 14-lb turkey equates to 13 × 14 = 182 minutes, or roughly 3 hours. I like to add 15 extra minutes to brown each side of the turkey, for a total of 3½ hours.

If using an instant-read meat thermometer: Insert the thermometer into the thickest part of the turkey thigh. When the thermometer reads 165°F, the turkey is ready to be removed from the oven.

To flip a turkey: Remove the roasting pan from the oven and set it down on a heat-safe countertop. Put on oven mitts and place a large freezer bag over each mitt. With your protected hands, carefully lift the turkey and flip it over. Remove the freezer bags (save them for later) and return the turkey to the oven.

Resting the turkey: Cover the turkey with foil and allow it to rest. The juices have a chance to redistribute through the meat, resulting in juicy, tender turkey.

Cooked turkey can be sliced and stored in the refrigerator for 5 days or in the freezer for up to 2 months.

To reheat, bring the sliced turkey to room temperature and reheat, covered, in a 375°F oven for 4–6 minutes.

Some people get fancy when it comes to cooking steak, which is completely understandable. I'm just not one of them. In culinary school, I learned to cook steak by starting with a good-quality, marbled cut of meat—such as a rib eye, Denver, or club steak—and adding a little salt, pepper, and olive oil. That's it. You won't need much else, except for perhaps a nice malbec.

STEAK WITH SCALLIONS, SESAME, AND MINT

READY IN 20 MINUTES

SERVES 4–6

Extra-virgin olive oil

3–4 (10-oz) strip steaks

Kosher salt and freshly ground black pepper

4 scallions, finely chopped

1 Tbsp sesame seeds

1 tsp finely chopped mint

SPECIAL TOOLS OR EQUIPMENT

Outdoor grill or indoor grill pan

Preheat an outdoor grill or indoor grill pan over high heat.

Drizzle a few drops of olive oil over the steaks, then season generously with salt and pepper.

Place the steaks on the grill and cook for 4–5 minutes until charred. Turn the steaks over and grill for another 5–6 minutes for medium or 8–10 minutes for medium-well. Transfer the steaks to a cutting board and cover loosely with aluminum foil. Set aside to rest for 5 minutes.

Meanwhile, in a small bowl, combine scallions, sesame seeds, and mint and mix well. Season with salt and pepper.

Using a chef's knife, slice the steaks across the grain into ¼-inch-thick slices (see tip below). Reserve the steak drippings.

Transfer the sliced steak onto a serving platter and spoon the drippings over top. Sprinkle the scallion mixture over the steak and serve immediately.

GOOD TO KNOW The white threads in the meat are the muscle fibers. When looking at a piece of meat, you can determine the direction of the fibers. Using a sharp knife, slice the meat perpendicular to the fibers. By cutting "against the grain," you shorten the fibers, making the meat easier to chew and more enjoyable to eat.

GET ORGANIZED Remove the steaks from the refrigerator about 20 minutes before you start cooking to bring them up to room temperature. This will result in juicier steak.

MAKE IT AHEAD Steak is best served immediately. If you plan to reheat and serve the steak later, undercook the steak for 4 minutes on each side.

STORAGE Steak with Scallions, Sesame, and Mint can be stored in the refrigerator for up to 4 days or in the freezer for up to 1 month.

REHEAT Bring the meat to room temperature and reheat, uncovered, in a 425°F oven for 5–7 minutes.

Roasts can serve a large crowd with minimal hassle. This coffee rub amplifies the meat's natural flavors while tenderizing it. I often cook a large roast, slice it, and freeze the slices in small batches to use in gourmet sandwiches.

PERFECT COFFEE-RUBBED ROAST

READY IN 3 HOURS AND 15 MINUTES

SERVES 8

COFFEE RUB

¼ cup ground espresso

2 Tbsp brown sugar

1 Tbsp paprika

1 Tbsp garlic powder

2 tsp kosher salt

1 tsp freshly ground black pepper

½ tsp ground cumin

ROAST

1 (4–5-lb) French (brick) roast

1 qty Coffee Rub (see here)

2 Tbsp light olive oil

2 yellow onions, thinly sliced

1 cup dry red wine

1 cup beef or chicken stock

SPECIAL TOOLS OR EQUIPMENT

Electric knife or chef's knife

Large roasting pan

COFFEE RUB In a small bowl, combine all ingredients and mix well.

ROAST Preheat oven to 325°F.

Pat the roast dry with paper towels. Sprinkle Coffee Rub all over the roast. Using your hands, press the rub into the roast and coat it completely.

Heat olive oil in a large roasting pan on the stovetop over medium-high heat. Add the roast and sear for 4 minutes per side, until browned. Transfer the roast to a cutting board and set aside.

Add onions to the pan and sauté for 8–10 minutes, until translucent and slightly browned. Place the roast on top of the onions. Pour wine and stock over the roast and bring to a boil. Loosely cover the pan with aluminum foil and roast for 2 ½ hours, until the roast is fork tender.

Transfer the roast to a cutting board and cover loosely with aluminum foil. Set aside for 10–15 minutes.

Meanwhile, place the roasting pan on the stovetop and cook the liquid and onions over medium-high heat for 5 minutes, until reduced and thickened.

Using a chef's knife or an electric knife, slice the roast into ⅛-inch-thick slices. Transfer to a serving platter, then spoon the sauce and onions on top. Serve immediately.

MAKE IT AHEAD Perfect Coffee-Rubbed Roast can be rubbed and marinated in advance and stored for up to 3 days in the refrigerator. Set the roast aside at room temperature for 1–2 hours before roasting. This ensures a juicy roast.

GOOD TO KNOW Dry red wines do not have any residual sugar and are less sweet than regular red wines. Look for a cabernet sauvignon, malbec, merlot, pinot noir, or shiraz.

REHEAT To reheat, bring the Perfect Coffee-Rubbed Roast to room temperature, cover, and reheat in a 350°F oven for about 10 minutes.

The "lollipop" short rib describes a cut of meat that has been separated from the bone. The meat is then trimmed of fat, wrapped around the base of the bone, and secured with twine to resemble a lollipop. Slow-braised over a low heat and smothered in a rich red–shallot sauce, these fall-off-the-bone ribs will change the way you think about "lollipops" forever.

SLOW-COOKED LOLLIPOP SHORT RIBS

READY IN 2 ½–3 HOURS

SERVES 4–6

4 beef lollipop short ribs

Kosher salt and freshly ground black pepper

¼ cup light olive oil (divided)

6 shallots, thinly sliced

2 cloves garlic, minced

1 (6-oz) can tomato paste

1 Tbsp brown sugar

2 cups chicken or vegetable stock

1 cup dry red wine

1 (14 ½-oz) can diced tomatoes

3 sprigs rosemary

SPECIAL TOOLS OR EQUIPMENT
Large roasting pan (optional)

Generously season ribs with salt and pepper.

In a large roasting pan or cast-iron skillet, heat 2 tablespoons olive oil over medium-high heat. Add ribs and sear for 5 minutes, turning occasionally, until all sides are browned. Transfer ribs to a baking sheet and set aside.

Heat the remaining 2 tablespoons of olive oil in the roasting pan over medium-high heat. Add shallots and sauté for 5 minutes. Add garlic and sauté for 1 minute. Stir in tomato paste and brown sugar, scraping up any of the burnt bits from the bottom of the pan.

Return the ribs to the pan. Pour stock, wine, and diced tomatoes over top. Add rosemary and bring to a boil. Reduce heat to low, cover, and slow-cook for 2–2 ½ hours, basting occasionally, until the meat is easily pierced with a fork.

Transfer ribs to a plate and set aside. Discard rosemary.

Bring the sauce in the roasting pan to a boil over medium-high heat and gently boil for 6–8 minutes, until reduced and thickened to your liking. Return ribs to the pan and spoon the sauce over top.

Transfer ribs to a serving platter and serve immediately.

GOOD TO KNOW Dry red wines do not have any residual sugar and are less sweet than regular red wines. Look for a cabernet sauvignon, malbec, merlot, pinot noir, or shiraz.

MAKE IT AHEAD Slow-Cooked Lollipop Short Ribs can be prepared in advance and stored in the refrigerator for up to 4 days or in the freezer for up to 1 month.

REHEAT Bring the Slow-Cooked Lollipop Short Ribs to room temperature. Reheat on the stovetop for 10–12 minutes over medium heat.

This hearty one-pot wonder is a reliable year-round dish that I serve with chunks of fresh, crusty baguette. These kefta (or oval-shaped meatballs) are studded with caramelized onions and then combined with edamame and peas.

BEEF KEFTA WITH EDAMAME AND ENGLISH PEAS

READY IN 40–45 MINUTES

SERVES 6

2 Tbsp light olive oil, plus extra for greasing

1 large onion, thinly sliced

2 lbs medium ground beef

½ cup breadcrumbs

3 Tbsp finely chopped flat-leaf parsley

2 Tbsp ketchup

1 tsp onion powder

1 tsp garlic powder

¼ tsp ground cinnamon

½ tsp kosher salt

¼ tsp freshly ground black pepper

1 cup shelled frozen edamame

1 cup frozen peas

Line a baking sheet with parchment paper.

Heat olive oil in a large nonstick skillet over medium heat. Add onion and sauté for 5–7 minutes, until softened and translucent. Keep warm on low heat.

In a large bowl, combine beef, breadcrumbs, parsley, ketchup, onion powder, garlic powder, cinnamon, salt, and pepper. Using your hands, mix the ingredients.

With oiled hands, roll 3 tablespoons of the meat mixture into an oval shape. Place on the prepared baking sheet. Repeat with the remaining mixture.

Heat the pan of sautéed onions over medium-high heat. Once the pan is hot, add the kefta and cook for 5 minutes on each side, until browned. Cover, reduce heat to medium, and cook for another 10 minutes.

Add edamame and peas and give the pan a good shake. Cover and cook for another 5 minutes.

GOOD TO KNOW Frozen peas and edamame do not need to be cooked—I promise! Simply thaw at room temperature or overnight in your refrigerator and run under cold water before serving.

SUBSTITUTIONS Kefta can also be made with ground chicken, turkey, lamb, or veal.

MAKE IT AHEAD The kefta meat mixture may also be frozen before cooking. Form the kefta into patties, then freeze them on a parchment-lined baking sheet for 1–2 hours, until frozen. Transfer the kefta to a freezer bag and store them in the freezer for up to 1 month. When ready to serve, simply thaw and cook as per instructions.

STORAGE Beef Kefta with Edamame and English Peas can be stored in the refrigerator for up to 3 days or in the freezer for up to 1 month.

REHEAT Bring to room temperature and reheat on the stovetop over medium heat for 8–10 minutes or in a 350°F oven for 7–10 minutes.

This is my family's favorite dinner request, be it a birthday or the Jewish new year. Served with lemon wedges and peppery arugula greens, these crispy yet tender veal cutlets make an impressive dish to mark an occasion.

VEAL MILANESE WITH LEMON AND ARUGULA

READY IN 45 MINUTES

SERVES 6

6 bone-in veal cutlets, pounded very thinly (I prefer rib-eye)

Kosher salt and freshly ground black pepper

3 eggs

1 tsp water

3 cups seasoned breadcrumbs (I prefer Israeli-style)

¾ cup neutral oil such as avocado oil, vegetable oil, or rice bran oil (divided)

2 lemons, cut into wedges

1 bunch peppery arugula, cleaned and dried

Using a paper towel, pat dry the veal cutlets. Generously season both sides with salt and pepper.

In a large baking dish, combine eggs, water, and a pinch of salt. Mix well.

Pour breadcrumbs into a separate large baking dish and place it next to the egg mixture.

Have 2 baking sheets ready. Hold a cutlet by the bone and dip the meaty part into the egg mixture, soaking it completely. Lift the cutlet out of the egg mixture and shake off the excess moisture. Place the cutlet into the breadcrumbs and coat completely on both sides. Transfer the breaded cutlet to a baking sheet. Repeat with the remaining cutlets.

Heat ¼ cup of oil in a very large nonstick skillet over medium-high heat, until hot but not smoking. (If the pan begins to smoke, remove it from the heat for 2–3 minutes to cool off. Return the pan to the burner and reduce the heat.) Working in batches to avoid overcrowding, place 2 cutlets into the pan and sauté for 6 minutes on each side, until crisp and golden. Transfer the cooked cutlets to a clean baking sheet. Repeat with the remaining cutlets, adding more oil as needed (there should be about ¼ cup of oil in the pan to cook 2 cutlets).

Arrange cutlets on a large platter or individual dinner plates, garnish with a few lemon wedges, and serve with a mound of arugula. Serve immediately.

GOOD TO KNOW "Overcrowding the pan" refers to adding too many ingredients to a pan at once. When the pan is overcrowded, too much steam is created, and instead of the food frying or searing, it steam-cooks and turns soggy.

I often use leftover bread to make crispy croutons. This salad is what I like to call my "surplus repurposed" salad. It's a clever and delicious way to repurpose all of my leftovers to create something amazing!

SHAWARMA SALAD WITH ZA'ATAR CROUTONS AND TAHINI

READY IN 25 MINUTES

SERVES 6

2–3 cups cubed bread (such as pita, challah, or bagels), room temperature, cut into ½-inch cubes

⅓–½ cup extra-virgin olive oil

¼ cup za'atar

Kosher salt and freshly ground black pepper

5 cups shredded romaine lettuce

1 cup halved cherry tomatoes

1 English cucumber, unpeeled and sliced into rounds

6 Israeli pickles, sliced into thin rounds

1 cup pitted black olives

¼ cup finely chopped flat-leaf parsley

2–3 cups shredded leftover chicken or turkey

½ cup tahini

¼ cup warm water

Juice of 1 lemon

1 clove garlic, minced

SPECIAL TOOLS OR EQUIPMENT
Glass jar

Preheat oven to 375°F. Line a baking sheet with parchment paper.

Place bread on the prepared baking sheet. Drizzle olive oil and sprinkle za'atar over top. Season with salt and pepper, and toss well. Bake for 10 minutes. Give the pan a good shake (so the edges don't burn), then bake for another 10 minutes, until bread is crisp and toasty. Remove from the oven and set aside.

Assemble the salad in individual salad bowls or on a large serving platter. Place lettuce at the base, then top with tomatoes, cucumber, pickles, olives, and parsley. Add croutons and chicken (or turkey).

In a glass jar, combine tahini, water, lemon juice, and garlic. Secure lid, then shake well to combine. Generously season with salt and pepper.

Drizzle the tahini mixture over the salad (2–3 tablespoons each for individual bowls or ½ cup for the salad platter). Serve immediately.

This recipe's super-easy marinade comes together in minutes! Orange and sage make a fantastic combo, but an unexpected introduction of wine and honey elevates flavor to new heights. Sometimes I'll throw the whole orange, unpeeled, into the food processor—it adds vibrant color and just the right amount of bitterness.

LAMB CHOPS WITH CITRUS AND SAGE

READY IN 40 MINUTES

SERVES 5

10 small lamb chops, Frenched

Kosher salt and freshly ground black pepper

1 small orange or clementine, peeled and pitted

1 clove garlic, peeled

Handful of sage

¼ cup white wine

1 Tbsp extra-virgin olive oil

1 tsp honey

Lightly dressed salad, to serve

SPECIAL TOOLS OR EQUIPMENT

Food processor or blender

Outdoor grill or indoor grill pan

Generously season lamb chops with salt and pepper. Transfer lamb chops to a large baking dish or a large freezer bag.

In a food processor or blender, combine orange, garlic, sage, wine, olive oil, and honey. Blitz together for 20 seconds, until orange is chunky and garlic is minced.

Pour the marinade over the lamb chops and marinate for 20 minutes at room temperature or up to 24 hours in the refrigerator. If marinating for more than 20 minutes, cover the baking dish tightly with plastic wrap or seal the freezer bag.

Preheat an outdoor grill or indoor grill pan over medium-high heat. Remove the lamb chops from the marinade and wipe off excess. Working in batches if necessary, place them on the grill. Grill the lamb chops for 2 minutes, until nicely browned. Flip the lamb chops over and cook for another 3 minutes for medium-rare or 3½ minutes for medium. (If you prefer your lamb cooked medium-well, transfer the lamb chops to an ovenproof dish and cook, uncovered, in a 375°F oven for another 3–5 minutes. If you are making this dish ahead of time, save this step until just before serving.)

Pour the remaining marinade into a small saucepan. Bring it to a boil over medium-high heat and continue boiling for another 3–4 minutes. Spoon the sauce over the lamb chops and serve immediately with a side of salad.

GOOD TO KNOW Should marinade be discarded after it's been used to marinate meat? If the marinade has boiled for 3–4 minutes, it can be reused as a sauce for cooked meat.

REHEAT Bring the lamb chops to room temperature, cover, and reheat in a 375°F oven for 4–6 minutes.

VEGETABLES AND SIDES

Think of a recipe as a general set of guidelines, not a letter of the law.

STYLING TIP

Take advantage of glass jars and loose vessels occupying space (or cupboards!) around your home. Even simply colored bottles can make a great statement. You can add votive candles or decorative ornaments or fill the vessels with water and freshly cut flowers.

This family favorite side dish is a simple yet effective way to jazz up basmati rice. This gorgeous golden rice cake is inverted onto a serving platter, showcasing the highly prized crunchy *tahdig* (the scorched crust), and sprinkled with chopped scallions. For a festive touch, garnish with pomegranate seeds, freshly chopped mint, and parsley.

CRISPY MUSHROOM RICE

READY IN 35 MINUTES,
PLUS 30 MINUTES SOAKING TIME

SERVES 8

2 cups basmati rice

¼ cup light olive oil (divided)

1 yellow onion, thinly sliced

2 cups assorted sliced mushrooms, gently wiped with damp paper towel

4 cups cold water, to cook rice

2 Tbsp kosher salt, plus extra to season

Freshly ground black pepper

1 bunch scallions, finely chopped

GOOD TO KNOW The best way to clean mushrooms is not to clean them at all. In fact, most mushrooms that you buy from the supermarket are grown indoors, not harvested in the wild. However, if you do notice any bits of dirt, simply wipe them away with a damp paper towel.

GOOD TO KNOW Soaking basmati rice isn't mandatory, but I find that it produces a fluffier and tastier rice.

REHEAT Crispy Mushroom Rice should be served immediately, but leftover rice can be covered loosely with foil and reheated in a 350°F oven for about 10 minutes.

Place rice in a large bowl and cover with cold water. Set aside to soak for 30 minutes.

Meanwhile, heat 2 tablespoons of olive oil in a large nonstick skillet over medium-high heat. Add onion and sauté for 5–7 minutes, until translucent and slightly brown. Add mushrooms and sauté for another 7–10 minutes, until browned. Don't worry if mushrooms shrink. Transfer the onion-mushroom mixture to a plate and set aside.

Drain rice, then quickly rinse under cold running water. Place rice in a medium saucepan and add 4 cups of cold water. Add salt. Cook rice according to package directions. Set aside to cool completely.

Transfer rice to a large mixing bowl. Stir in the onion-mushroom mixture and season with salt and pepper.

Heat the remaining 2 tablespoons of olive oil in a nonstick skillet over medium-high heat. Once oil is hot, transfer the mushroom rice to the skillet and spread it out. Cook for 10 minutes. Using a wooden spoon, press down on the rice for 1–2 minutes to form a crusty base.

Invert the rice onto a serving platter. Scatter chopped scallions over top and serve immediately.

These are no ordinary roasted potatoes. Here, I've coupled Yukon Gold potatoes with onions and cooked them so that they taste both ridiculously crispy and melt-in-your-mouth tender at the same time. It's a simple recipe with an extraordinary outcome.

CRISPY POTATOES AND ONIONS

READY IN 50 MINUTES

SERVES 6

8 Yukon Gold potatoes, peeled and cut into 8 wedges

3 yellow onions, thinly sliced

¼ cup extra-virgin olive oil or schmaltz

2 Tbsp cornstarch

1 Tbsp dried parsley

1 tsp garlic powder

1 tsp kosher salt

½ tsp freshly ground black pepper

½ tsp ground turmeric

Preheat oven to 375°F.

Place potatoes and onions on a large baking sheet (or 2 smaller baking sheets) and cover tightly with aluminum foil. Bake for 15 minutes. (We steam-cook the potatoes to ensure they are cooked through before they're crisped up.) Remove from the oven, uncover, and set aside for 5 minutes.

Drizzle olive oil (or schmaltz) over potatoes and onions and toss to combine.

In a small bowl, combine cornstarch, parsley, garlic powder, salt, pepper, and turmeric. Sprinkle the mixture over the potatoes and onions and toss to coat.

Roast, uncovered, for 15 minutes. Give the baking sheet a good shake to loosen up the mixture and mix a bit. Bake for another 15 minutes, until crisp and golden. Serve immediately.

GOOD TO KNOW The cornstarch coating boosts the potatoes and onions with additional crisp and crunch.

GET ORGANIZED To crisp up potatoes and onions to perfection, it is crucial not to overcrowd the pan. Overcrowding will only result in mushy potatoes and onions, which is not the outcome we want.

REHEAT Crispy Potatoes and Onions can be reheated, uncovered, in a 350°F oven for 10 minutes.

Savory, sweet, salty, and deliciously satisfying—you cannot go wrong with this recipe. Traditionally, ramen noodles are had in the eponymous noodle dish. I pan-fry them here with lots of veggies and crushed peanuts for an equally flavorful broth-less option.

VEGETABLE RAMEN WITH SOY-GARLIC SAUCE AND PEANUTS

READY IN 35 MINUTES

SERVES 6

SOY-GARLIC SAUCE

½ cup soy sauce

3 Tbsp rice vinegar

3 Tbsp mirin

1 Tbsp brown sugar or coconut sugar

1 Tbsp grated ginger

1 Tbsp toasted sesame oil

VEGETABLE RAMEN

1 (9½-oz) package ramen wheat noodles

2 Tbsp neutral oil such as avocado oil, vegetable oil, or rice bran oil

1 yellow onion, thinly sliced

1 clove garlic, minced

1 jalapeño or cayenne pepper, seeded, deveined, and thinly sliced (optional)

3 carrots, julienned

1 head broccoli, cut into florets

1 cup snow peas, trimmed

1 bunch scallions, trimmed and finely chopped

Kosher salt and freshly ground black pepper

¼ cup crushed roasted and salted peanuts, plus extra to serve

Chili oil, to serve

SOY-GARLIC SAUCE In a small saucepan, combine all ingredients except sesame oil and mix well. Cook over medium heat for 7 minutes, stir continuously, until the sugar dissolves and the mixture comes to a slow simmer. Remove from heat, then stir in sesame oil. Set aside to cool.

VEGETABLE RAMEN Cook ramen noodles according to package directions. Drain, then set aside.

Heat oil in a large nonstick skillet over medium-high heat. Add onion, garlic, and jalapeño (or cayenne), if using, and sauté for 5–7 minutes, until browned. Add carrots, broccoli, snow peas, and scallions and sauté for another 7 minutes.

Add ramen noodles to the skillet and stir into the vegetables. Season with salt and pepper. Pour the soy-garlic sauce over the ramen and vegetables and toss well. Cook for 5 minutes.

Transfer to a serving platter, top with crushed peanuts, and serve immediately with extra peanuts and chili oil on the side.

GOOD TO KNOW Mirin is a sweet rice wine with a syrupy texture. Used in Japanese cooking, it adds depth and richness to a dish.

SUBSTITUTIONS Ramen noodles can be replaced with udon noodles.

I was raised on my mother's traditional Moroccan cooking, much of which was flavored with aromatic saffron. However, it wasn't until I was in my thirties that I discovered the divine combination of saffron and yogurt. Here, earthy saffron cream sits atop lusciously caramelized baby yams, creating the perfect bite.

BABY YAMS WITH SAFFRON CREAM

12 baby yams, scrubbed and dried

Extra-virgin olive oil, for drizzling

Kosher salt and freshly ground black pepper

4 threads saffron

1 tsp boiling water

1 cup plain yogurt or dairy-free yogurt

2 tsp finely chopped mint leaves

Preheat oven to 375°F. Cut 12 (5-inch) square pieces of aluminum foil.

Place a yam on a small square of aluminum foil. Drizzle with ¼ teaspoon of olive oil and sprinkle with salt and pepper. Wrap the yam in the foil. Repeat with the remaining yams.

Place the foil-wrapped yams on a baking sheet and bake for 30–40 minutes, until they can be easily pierced with a fork.

Meanwhile, combine saffron and boiling water in a small bowl and mix. Set aside for 1 minute. Stir in yogurt, then season with salt and pepper.

Remove the yams from the oven and set aside until cool enough to handle. Unwrap each one. Using a sharp knife, cut a slit into the top of each yam.

Transfer the yams to a serving platter, dollop a teaspoon of saffron cream on top of each, then sprinkle chopped mint and a little extra pepper over top. Serve immediately with the remaining saffron cream.

MAKE IT AHEAD Saffron Cream can be prepared up to 2 hours in advance and stored in the refrigerator. Stir well before serving.

MAKE IT AHEAD Baby yams can be cooked in the oven and kept wrapped in foil with the oven turned off for up to 2 hours in advance.

REHEAT To reheat, place the wrapped yams in a 375°F oven for 5–10 minutes.

This recipe may seem long, but it's only because I've included specific instructions for mastering three important kitchen techniques:

1. How to perfect jammy eggs;
2. How to master fried eggplant; and
3. How to whip up a beautiful herb oil in a matter of seconds.

These are skills you will use time and time again. You're welcome.

FRIED EGGPLANT AND JAMMY EGGS WITH HERB OIL

READY IN 20 MINUTES, PLUS 15 MINUTES RESTING TIME

SERVES 6

FRIED EGGPLANT AND JAMMY EGGS

1 eggplant

Kosher salt and freshly ground black pepper

6 cold eggs

¼ cup neutral oil such as avocado oil, vegetable oil, or rice bran oil (divided)

Bread, to serve

Spicy Green Tahini (p. 44), to serve

FRIED EGGPLANT AND JAMMY EGGS Line a baking sheet with parchment paper.

Using a chef's knife, slice eggplant into ¼-inch-thick slices. Place eggplant slices on the prepared baking sheet and sprinkle salt on both sides of the slices. Let eggplant rest for 15 minutes.

Meanwhile, bring a medium saucepan of cold water to a boil. Stir in a good pinch of salt.

Using a slotted spoon, gently lower a whole egg, one at a time, into the saucepan. (This prevents the shells from cracking when adding eggs into the boiling water.) Repeat with the remaining eggs. Reduce heat to medium-low and simmer for precisely 6½ minutes, uncovered.

Prepare an ice bath. Once eggs are cooked, use a slotted spoon to carefully transfer eggs into the ice bath. Set aside for exactly 2 minutes. Remove the eggs from the ice bath and carefully peel away the shells to maintain a smooth surface. Set eggs aside.

Use a paper towel to blot any liquid and salt from the eggplant slices.

HERB OIL

¼ cup extra-virgin olive oil

3 Tbsp finely chopped fresh
herbs of your choice, plus extra to
garnish

SPECIAL TOOLS OR EQUIPMENT

Squeeze bottle

Heat 3 tablespoons of neutral oil in a large nonstick skillet over
medium-high heat. Add the eggplant, 4–5 slices at a time, and
cook for 3 minutes on each side, until golden. Transfer to a serving
platter. Repeat with the remaining eggplant slices, adding more oil
if needed.

Cut the eggs in half lengthwise and arrange them on the platter.
Season with salt and pepper.

HERB OIL Combine olive oil and finely chopped fresh herbs in a
squeeze bottle and shake well. Alternatively, combine the olive oil
and herbs in a small bowl.

ASSEMBLY Squeeze or drizzle droplets of herb oil over the eggplant
and jammy eggs. Garnish with fresh herbs. Serve immediately with
bread and Spicy Green Tahini.

MAKE IT AHEAD Jammy Eggs can be
prepared and peeled in advance, left
whole, and stored in the refrigerator
for up to 2 days.

FRIED EGGPLANT
AND JAMMY EGGS
WITH HERB OIL

As a child, I would look forward to Shabbat dinner because there was always a mezze bowl of thinly sliced fennel with a splash of lemon juice and lots of black pepper on the table. Although I still opt to eat it raw, I have found that slow-cooking fennel is a fantastic way of switching it up and surprising my dinner guests.

SLOW-COOKED CARAMELIZED FENNEL

READY IN 1 HOUR

SERVES 4–6

3 Tbsp light olive oil (divided)

2 large yellow onions, halved widthwise

4 fennel bulbs, trimmed, thick outer layers removed, and quartered lengthwise

1 tsp kosher salt

¼ tsp freshly ground black pepper

¾ cup warm water

1 tsp ground ginger

½ tsp saffron

Grated zest of 1 orange

Juice of 1 lemon

2 Tbsp roughly chopped dill, for garnish

Preheat oven to 400°F.

Heat 2 tablespoons olive oil in a Dutch oven or deep ovenproof skillet over medium-high heat. Add onions and fennel, cut-side down, so that they fit snugly. Season with salt and pepper. Cook for 10 minutes, uncovered and untouched.

In a small bowl, combine water, ginger, saffron, and orange zest. Pour mixture over the fennel and onions and cover. Transfer pan into the oven and cook, covered, for 20 minutes. Baste, then cover and return to the oven. Braise for another 20 minutes. Remove pot from the oven and set aside for 3 minutes.

Top with lemon juice and dill. Serve immediately.

GOOD TO KNOW To "braise" is to cook in sauce at a low temperature.

REHEAT Slow-Cooked Caramelized Fennel is best served immediately, but it can be covered loosely with aluminum foil and reheated in a 350°F oven for 10 minutes until warmed through.

This super-simple cauliflower dish always gets rave reviews. Instead of serving the cauliflower in its typical floret form, try roasting thickly sliced cauliflower until crisp. Sprinkled with za'atar and a little salt and pepper, it's insanely good.

ZA'ATAR CAULIFLOWER STEAKS

READY IN 25 MINUTES

SERVES 6

1 head cauliflower, leaves removed, rinsed and dried

Kosher salt and freshly ground black pepper

¼ cup extra-virgin olive oil

3 Tbsp za'atar

Preheat oven to 375°F. Line a large baking sheet with parchment paper.

Trim the base of the cauliflower and set it on a cutting board. Using a chef's knife, slice cauliflower into 1-inch-thick slices. Place cauliflower steaks on the prepared baking sheet. Generously season with salt and pepper.

Drizzle with olive oil and sprinkle za'atar on top. Bake for 15–20 minutes, until crisp.

Transfer to a serving platter and serve immediately.

MAKE IT AHEAD The cauliflower can be trimmed and sliced in advance and stored in freezer bags in the refrigerator for up to 2 days.

REHEAT To reheat, place the cauliflower on a baking sheet and heat, uncovered, in a 350°F oven for 5 minutes.

It often amazes me to see how much my kids love broccoli—they devour it! This staple recipe is full of nutrients, has the perfect amount of crunch, and whips up in a flash. Plus, the key is to burn the broccoli, so you cannot mess this up!

CHARRED BROCCOLI AND GARLIC

READY IN 10–15 MINUTES

SERVES 6

1 head broccoli, cut into florets

2 Tbsp extra-virgin olive oil

2 cloves garlic, thinly sliced

Kosher salt and freshly ground black pepper

SPECIAL TOOLS OR EQUIPMENT

Indoor grill pan or cast-iron skillet

Heat an indoor grill pan or a cast-iron skillet over medium-high heat. Add the broccoli florets and grill, covered, for 2 minutes, just until the broccoli turns bright green.

Drizzle olive oil over the florets, add garlic, and generously season with salt and pepper. Increase the heat to high and cook broccoli for 4–6 minutes, until all sides are charred.

Transfer to a serving platter and serve immediately.

I've always enjoyed asparagus topped with fried eggs and shaved truffles in restaurants around the world; then, it occurred to me that I could re-create this at home. I'll show you how easy it can be with this simple recipe.

ASPARAGUS WITH EGGS, TRUFFLE OIL, AND PARMESAN

READY IN 15 MINUTES

SERVES 4–6

1 bunch asparagus, cleaned and trimmed

2 tsp extra-virgin olive oil (divided)

Kosher salt and freshly ground black pepper

4–6 eggs

½ tsp truffle oil

2 Tbsp shaved Parmesan cheese

Slice each asparagus spear in half lengthwise.

Heat 1 teaspoon of olive oil in a large nonstick skillet over medium-high heat. Add asparagus, cover, and cook for 1 minute. Season with salt and pepper, then cook for another 3 minutes, until tender. Transfer asparagus to a serving platter.

Add the remaining 1 teaspoon of olive oil to the skillet and reduce heat to medium. One at a time, crack the eggs into a small bowl, then gently add to the hot oil. Fry for 5 minutes.

Gently place the fried eggs over the asparagus. Drizzle truffle oil over the eggs, then top with shaved Parmesan and black pepper. Serve immediately.

GOOD TO KNOW Most truffle oils on the market are *not* made with actual truffles. Instead, a product is used to mimic the taste of truffles, often resulting in a pungent, overpowering smell. It is essential to use truffle oil made with actual truffles, so please check the ingredients. My favorite brand is TruffleHunter.

Breakfast, lunch, or dinner—this recipe can be enjoyed any time of day. Crispy, golden, onion-y hash browns, accentuated with bright, trickling, fried eggs, this is a dish you will eat right out of the pan. No leftovers, I guarantee it.

HASH BROWNS AND EGGS

READY IN 30 MINUTES

SERVES 6

4 russet potatoes, peeled

2 yellow onions

Kosher salt and freshly ground black pepper

2 Tbsp light olive oil

6 eggs

2 Tbsp finely chopped dill

SPECIAL TOOLS OR EQUIPMENT

Box grater (or the grater setting of your food processor, but it won't be as good)

Using a box grater, coarsely grate potatoes and onions. Use your hands to squeeze out the excess liquid and discard. Place the grated potato and onion in a bowl and mix together, then generously season with salt and pepper.

Heat olive oil in a large nonstick skillet over medium-high heat. Add the potato-onion mixture and spread out into an even layer. Press down lightly with a spatula, then cover and cook for 5 minutes. Uncover and sauté for another 5 minutes, until golden brown on all sides.

Using the spatula, break up the hash browns and make 6 openings in the mixture. Crack an egg into each well, cover, and cook for 3 minutes, just until eggs turn opaque. Uncover eggs, season with salt and pepper, and sprinkle dill over top. Cook for another 2–3 minutes.

Transfer to a serving platter and serve immediately.

Some of the best mashed potatoes are loaded with butter and heavy cream, but you can make an equally delicious dairy-free version that won't compromise flavor. The star of this show is the caramelized onion. Laced in mashed potatoes, the puréed "onion crème" imparts an intense creaminess and a pronounced depth of flavor.

MASHED POTATOES WITH ONION CRÈME

READY IN 40 MINUTES

SERVES 6

2 Tbsp light olive oil

3 yellow onions, thinly sliced

8 Yukon Gold potatoes, scrubbed, peeled, and quartered

½ tsp kosher salt, plus extra to season

Freshly ground black pepper

2–3 Tbsp extra-virgin olive oil

SPECIAL TOOLS OR EQUIPMENT

Food processor or blender

Potato masher

Heat the light olive oil in a large nonstick skillet over medium-high heat. Add onions and reduce heat to medium. Sauté for 10–15 minutes, until softened and caramelized. Set aside to cool.

Transfer onions to a food processor or blender and purée for 1–2 minutes, until smooth. Transfer to a small bowl and set aside.

Place potatoes and salt in a medium saucepan and cover with cold water. Bring to a boil over high heat, then reduce heat to medium. Cover and cook for 15–20 minutes, until they can be easily pierced with a fork. Drain.

Return potatoes to the saucepan and cook over medium heat for 2 minutes. This is called "pan-drying." Stir in the onion crème, then mash the potatoes and onions together. Season generously with salt and pepper and mix.

Drizzle the extra-virgin olive oil over the mashed potatoes and serve immediately.

GOOD TO KNOW "Pan-drying" is a cooking technique where boiled potatoes are cooked in a dry pot for a few minutes to remove moisture and "dry out" the potatoes.

MAKE IT AHEAD Onions can be sautéed and puréed in advance and stored in the refrigerator for up to 7 days or in the freezer for up to 1 month.

MAKE IT AHEAD Potatoes are best mashed just after cooking and can be mashed 2 hours in advance of serving.

REHEAT Reheat mashed potatoes in a saucepan over medium heat for 5–10 minutes. You may need to drizzle a little extra-virgin olive oil for added creaminess.

A tagine is a traditional Moroccan cooking vessel made of ceramic or unglazed clay. The wide, shallow base allows for the release of a unique, slow-cooked flavor imparted by the ingredients and the clayware. The tagine doubles as both a cooking vessel and a serving dish that keeps the food warm.

If you don't have a tagine at home, you may cook this hearty dish in a Dutch oven.

LEEK, LENTIL, AND CHICKPEA TAGINE

READY IN 45 MINUTES

SERVES 4–6

2 Tbsp extra-virgin olive oil

3 leeks, white and light green parts only, roughly chopped

1 zucchini, cut into ¼-inch cubes

1 clove garlic, minced

½ tsp ground cumin

½ tsp ground coriander

1 (15 ½-oz) can chickpeas, drained and rinsed

½ cup brown lentils, rinsed

1 tsp kosher salt

¼ tsp freshly ground black pepper

1 ½ cups vegetable stock

A dollop of yogurt or ¼ cup crumbled feta cheese

¼ cup toasted pine nuts

Handful of flat-leaf parsley, chopped

SPECIAL TOOLS OR EQUIPMENT
Tagine or Dutch oven

Heat olive oil in a tagine or a Dutch oven over medium-high heat. Add leeks and zucchini and cook for 5 minutes, or until softened and lightly browned. Add garlic, cumin, and coriander and cook for another 2 minutes, until fragrant. Add chickpeas, lentils, salt, and pepper and mix well.

Pour in stock. Bring to a boil, then reduce heat to medium-low. Cover and simmer for 20–25 minutes, until all the liquid is absorbed.

Meanwhile, preheat oven to broil. Place the Dutch oven or tagine in the oven, uncovered, and broil for 1–2 minutes, until the surface crisps up. Watch this carefully to prevent the top from burning.

Top with yogurt (or feta), pine nuts, and parsley. Serve immediately.

REHEAT Leek, Lentil, and Chickpea Tagine is best served immediately, but it can be covered loosely with aluminum foil and reheated in a 350°F oven for about 10 minutes.

LEFTOVER MAKEOVER

If you've ever wondered what to do with all the leftovers in the refrigerator, this section is for you! Here are a few creative reinventions for leftovers, giving them new life while minimizing waste.

ARAYES (GRILLED STUFFED PITA)

READY IN 15 MINUTES

SERVES 6

1 tomato

3–4 cups sliced or shredded leftover beef or lamb, room temperature

2 Tbsp finely chopped flat-leaf parsley

1 tsp finely chopped mint

Kosher salt and freshly ground black pepper

6 pitas, cut in half to create 12 pockets

2 Tbsp extra-virgin olive oil

1 lemon, cut into 8 wedges

SPECIAL TOOLS OR EQUIPMENT
Box grater
Outdoor grill or indoor grill pan

Prepare an ice bath.

Bring a saucepan of water to a boil. Using a sharp paring knife, remove the tomato stem and discard. Score an "X" shape at the base of the tomato. Gently lower the tomato into the boiling water and boil for 1 minute. Transfer the tomato to the ice bath and set aside for 1 minute. Once cool enough to handle, remove the skin starting from the base.

Using a box grater, coarsely grate tomato into a large bowl. Add beef (or lamb), parsley, and mint, and mix well. Season with salt and pepper.

Generously spoon mixture into each pita pocket, so the pita is filled. Repeat with the remaining pitas and filling.

Preheat an outdoor grill or indoor grill pan over medium-high heat. Brush olive oil on both sides of each pita. Place pitas on the hot grill and grill for 2 minutes on each side, until pitas are toasty and the filling is hot.

Serve immediately with lemon wedges.

TORTILLAS WITH SPICY HUMMUS

READY IN 15 MINUTES

SERVES 6

Cooking spray

½ cup hummus

½ tsp harissa

4 cups chopped leftover hamburger, meatballs, kefta, or meatloaf, room temperature

6 whole-wheat tortilla wraps, halved

SPECIAL TOOLS OR EQUIPMENT

Outdoor grill or indoor grill pan

Preheat an outdoor grill or indoor grill pan over medium-high heat. Lightly grease the grill or grill pan with cooking spray.

Combine hummus and harissa in a small bowl and mix well. Set aside.

Spoon the meat filling into the center of the tortilla. Roll it up tightly, tucking in the sides as you roll (fold one side in, and then the other). With both ends folded, tightly roll up the tortilla. Repeat with the remaining tortillas.

Place 2–3 tortillas, seam-side down, onto the hot grill. Cook for 2–3 minutes on each side, making sure that grill marks appear. (The heat and grease will seal the seam shut.) Repeat with the remaining tortillas.

Slice diagonally in half and dollop spicy hummus on top. Serve immediately.

CRISPY SPAGHETTI PIE

READY IN 35 MINUTES

SERVES 6

1 (16-oz) package spaghetti

1 (6-oz) can tomato paste

½ tsp ground cinnamon

½ tsp ground allspice

½ tsp kosher salt

¼ tsp freshly ground black pepper

2 cups shredded leftover chicken, turkey, or beef, skin and bones removed

2 Tbsp light olive oil

Cook the pasta in salted water according to package directions. Drain spaghetti, reserving ½ cup of cooking liquid.

In a large bowl, combine spaghetti, the reserved cooking liquid, tomato paste, cinnamon, allspice, salt, and pepper. Add the shredded meat and mix well.

Heat olive oil in a large, deep nonstick skillet over medium-high heat. Spoon the spaghetti mixture into the pan. Using a spatula, pack the spaghetti into the pan and firmly press in. Reduce to medium heat, cover, and cook for 15 minutes. Remove from heat and set aside for 10 minutes.

Invert spaghetti pie onto a serving platter and serve immediately.

PENNE WITH TOMATOES, GARLIC, AND KALE

READY IN 25 MINUTES

SERVES 6

1 (16-oz) box penne pasta

1 Tbsp light olive oil

1 pint cherry tomatoes

4 cloves garlic, minced

1 tsp chili flakes

2–3 cups shredded leftover chicken, beef, or flaked skinless fish

2 cups kale leaves

¼ cup chopped basil leaves

2 tsp extra-virgin olive oil

Kosher salt and freshly ground black pepper

Cook the penne according to package directions (be sure to salt your water). Drain pasta, reserving ½ cup of the cooking liquid. Transfer penne into a large bowl and set aside.

Heat the light olive oil in a large nonstick skillet over medium-high heat. Add tomatoes and cook for 4 minutes, shaking the skillet periodically, until the tomatoes "blitz and pop." (Be careful as the oil can burn! Reduce heat if necessary.) Add garlic and chili flakes and cook for 2 minutes, until golden.

Stir in the chicken (or beef or fish) and cook for another 3 minutes. Add kale and the reserved pasta cooking liquid and cook for another 2 minutes, until kale is wilted. Add penne and stir. Remove from heat. Finish with basil and extra-virgin olive oil and toss well. Generously season with salt and pepper.

Transfer to a serving platter and serve immediately.

FLATBREAD WITH SUMAC ONIONS

READY IN 15 MINUTES

SERVES 6

1 red onion, thinly sliced

¼–½ cup extra-virgin olive oil

1 Tbsp red wine vinegar

2 tsp sumac

2–3 cups sliced cooked chicken or steak

6 flatbreads

½ cup hummus

Kosher salt and freshly ground black pepper

SPECIAL TOOLS OR EQUIPMENT
Outdoor grill or indoor grill pan

Preheat oven to 350°F.

Place onion in a shallow bowl. Add enough olive oil to nearly cover onion. Add vinegar and sumac and mix well. Set aside for 10 minutes.

Transfer chicken (or steak) to a baking sheet, cover with aluminum foil, and warm in the oven for 5–10 minutes until hot.

Meanwhile, preheat an outdoor grill or indoor grill pan over high heat. Place flatbreads on the grill or pan and heat for 1 minute on each side, until hot.

Spread a thin layer of hummus over each flatbread. Transfer to a serving platter, then arrange the chicken (or steak) on top, and finish with red onions and a generous drizzle of onion marinade. Season with salt and pepper. Serve immediately.

RICE BOWLS WITH FISH AND HONEY-LIME DRIZZLE

READY IN 15–20 MINUTES

SERVES 6

HONEY-LIME SAUCE

Juice of 2 limes (about ¼ cup)

1 Tbsp honey

1 tsp soy sauce

1 Tbsp neutral oil such as avocado oil, vegetable oil, or rice bran oil

1 clove garlic, minced

1 tsp grated ginger

2 Tbsp chopped fresh herbs (such as cilantro, parsley, and/or basil)

Kosher salt and freshly ground black pepper

RICE BOWLS

3 cups steamed (or cooked) rice, hot or room temperature

2 cups leftover skinless flaked fish, room temperature

2 carrots, julienned

2 cups shredded red cabbage

2 avocados, thinly sliced

4 scallions, trimmed and finely chopped

1 Tbsp black sesame seeds

1 Tbsp white sesame seeds

Sriracha or sliced chiles (optional)

HONEY-LIME SAUCE In a small jar, combine all ingredients, secure lid, and shake well. Set aside.

RICE BOWLS Scoop ½ cup of rice into each bowl. Add ⅓ cup flaked fish, carrots, red cabbage, and avocado. Scatter scallions on top and sprinkle with sesame seeds. Add a little Sriracha (or sliced chiles), if using. Spoon the honey-lime sauce over each bowl.

Serve immediately.

SWEETS

How a meal ends is as important as how it starts.

STYLING TIP

Fresh fruit such as grapes, figs, cherries, and pomegranates can enhance the mood with deep colors. Instead of flowers, decorate the run of your table with fruit that looks beautiful and tastes delicious as well.

What in God's name is pistachio dust? Exactly as it sounds. Pistachios are chopped ultrafine until they transform into a bright green magical dust that adds incredible flavor to ordinary foods such as oranges and grapefruit. Sometimes the simplest desserts are the most loved.

SLICED CITRUS WITH PISTACHIO DUST

READY IN 15 MINUTES

SERVES 6

6–8 assorted citrus fruits (oranges, clementines, tangerines, grapefruit, or pomelos)

¼ cup shelled and unsalted roasted pistachios, ultrafinely chopped

Using a sharp knife, slice off the top and bottom of the citrus fruit, just far enough to expose the flesh. Place the fruit, cut-side down, so that it is sturdy on your cutting board. Cut away the peel and as much of the white pith as possible by following the citrus's shape. Turn the fruit on its side and slice into ⅛-inch-thick slices. Repeat with the remaining citrus.

Arrange the citrus on a large platter, slightly overlapping. Sprinkle 1–2 tablespoons of pistachio dust over the citrus slices. Serve immediately.

MAKE IT AHEAD The citrus fruit can be sliced in advance, covered, and stored for up to 3 hours in the refrigerator. Sprinkle the pistachio dust just before serving.

STORAGE Pistachio dust can be stored in a small glass jar in your pantry or freezer for up to 3 months.

My ideal dessert has three elements: wine, berries, and chocolate. Here, juicy berries are macerated (soaked) in red wine and mint, then topped with dark chocolate curls to bring out a surprising richness and sophistication in this luscious dessert.

WINE, BERRIES, AND CHOCOLATE

READY IN 10 MINUTES, PLUS 2 HOURS SOAKING TIME

SERVES 6–8

4–6 cups assorted berries (strawberries, raspberries, blackberries, blueberries), cleaned and trimmed

1 cup dry red wine

4 mint leaves, finely chopped

1 (3-oz) bar high-quality dark chocolate, at least 70% cocoa

Place freezer-safe bowls or cups in the freezer for at least 1 hour before using.

If using strawberries, halve them into bite-sized pieces. In a large bowl, combine berries, wine, and mint and gently toss together. Soak for 2 hours.

Divide berries and wine into 6–8 individual chilled serving bowls or cups. Using a vegetable peeler, shave 1–2 tablespoons of chocolate over each bowl. Serve immediately.

GOOD TO KNOW Dry red wines do not have any residual sugar and are less sweet than regular red wines. Look for a cabernet sauvignon, malbec, merlot, pinot noir, or syrah/shiraz.

MAKE IT AHEAD Wine, Berries, and Chocolate can be prepared up to 4 hours in advance. Cover and refrigerate in a large bowl. Stir gently before dividing into individual serving bowls or cups. Add the shaved chocolate just before serving.

This easy recipe makes the most of berries on their way out. Any assortment of berries may be used (frozen berries will work as well): simply blitz them with your favorite wine and lots of ice, and you'll be happier in just minutes.

BERRY FROSÉ

READY IN 5–10 MINUTES

SERVES 4–6

2 cups assorted berries

1 (750-mL) bottle rosé wine

2 cups ice

Fresh mint or basil leaves, for garnish

Place the berries, rosé, and ice into a blender. Blend on high speed, until ice is slushy and ingredients are well incorporated.

Transfer to chilled glasses and garnish with mint (or basil).

GET ORGANIZED Chilling the glasses in the refrigerator or freezer for 30 minutes before serving keeps the frosé slushy and cool.

OPTIONAL Frosé can be served in chilled shot glasses as a fun party treat!

SUBSTITUTIONS Frosé can be made with white wine or moscato.

Traditionally called *rifat* or *les galettes*, these crispy, mildly sweet Moroccan biscuits are regarded as a digestif to be served with tea after a meal. For me, these anise seed biscuits taste of home, and my mother will bring over a giant container of these homemade treats whenever she visits. When I finally perfected these biscuits, it filled me with pride and joy to share a part of my childhood with my children.

MOROCCAN ANISE AND SESAME TEA BISCUITS

READY IN 35–40 MINUTES

MAKES ABOUT 5 DOZEN BISCUITS

1 cup orange juice

1 cup neutral oil such as avocado oil, vegetable oil, or rice bran oil

1 egg

1 tsp vanilla extract

4–5 cups all-purpose flour

1 cup sugar

½ cup cornstarch

1 tsp baking powder

3 Tbsp sesame seeds

2 Tbsp anise seed

A good pinch of kosher salt

Mint tea, to serve

SPECIAL TOOLS OR EQUIPMENT

4 baking sheets

Dough docker or fork

Fluted pastry wheel or regular knife

GET ORGANIZED By rolling out the dough onto parchment paper and baking the biscuits directly on the parchment, the cookies are handled less and the risk of breaking them is minimal.

STORAGE Moroccan Anise and Sesame Tea Biscuits can be stored in an airtight container for up to 2 months.

Preheat oven to 350°F.

In a stand mixer fitted with the paddle attachment (or using a hand-held mixer), combine orange juice, oil, egg, and vanilla. Beat on high speed for 2 minutes, until creamy. Add 4 cups flour, sugar, cornstarch, and baking powder. Mix on low speed until combined and a soft, pliable dough forms. If tacky, add more flour as needed, ¼ cup at a time, and mix on low. Add sesame seeds, anise seeds, and salt and mix on low until just combined.

Divide the dough into 4 equal-sized balls. Place a dough ball in between 2 large sheets of parchment paper. Roll out the dough into a rectangle with a thickness of ⅛ inch. Remove the top sheet of parchment paper and set aside.

Transfer the rolled-out dough *on* the parchment paper onto a baking sheet. Using a dough docker or a fork, pierce the dough all over. Using a fluted pastry wheel or regular knife, cut a grid shape onto the dough, creating biscuits of about 2 × 1 ½ inches. (The biscuit rectangles will not separate from the dough—the cutter perforates the dough and, once baked, the biscuits can break apart easily.) Gently pull away any leftover dough scraps around the border of the dough and re-roll to make more biscuits. Repeat the process with the remaining 3 dough balls.

Bake for 20–25 minutes, until golden brown, rotating the baking sheets midway through baking. Set aside to cool completely, then gently break apart the biscuits. Serve with mint tea.

These chewy, melt-in-your-mouth cookies started as a popular Passover recipe but soon became a year-round staple. I wish I could say this was an heirloom recipe passed down from generation to generation, but it was passed to me by my sister Jordana, who got this from her friend, who got it from her sister-in-law who... You get the picture.

CHEWY AND NUTTY FLOURLESS CHOCOLATE CHIP COOKIES

READY IN 20–25 MINUTES

MAKES ABOUT 2 DOZEN COOKIES

1 cup finely chopped walnuts

1 cup finely chopped pecans

¾ cup sugar

1 egg

1 Tbsp vanilla extract

Pinch of kosher salt

½ cup mini chocolate chips or finely chopped chocolate

Preheat oven to 350°F. Line 2 baking sheets with parchment paper.

In a medium bowl, combine nuts, sugar, egg, vanilla, and salt and mix well. Stir in the chocolate.

Using a small ice-cream scooper, scoop small mounds of the mixture onto the prepared baking sheets, evenly spacing them 2 inches apart. Bake for 15–20 minutes until lightly golden. Set aside to cool completely. The cookies will harden as they cool.

SUBSTITUTIONS You can use any combination of finely chopped nuts, but walnuts and pecans are my favorite.

STORAGE Chewy and Nutty Flourless Chocolate Chip Cookies can be stored in an airtight container for up to 5 days. They can also be frozen, in a single layer in a zip-top bag, for 1 month.

This wonderfully easy recipe salvages the most overripe fruit—it's what I call a "no-recipe recipe." Once you've taken command of the simple oat-crumb topping, you can add it to your repertoire and customize it with your favorite nuts and fruits. I grill the fruit to soften it and intensify flavors, but it also helps speed the cooking time. This satisfying crisp is made for cool-weather comfort.

QUICK FRUIT CRISP WITH OATS AND CINNAMON

READY IN 25–30 MINUTES

SERVES 6

5 cups sliced fruit of choice (such as peaches, plums, apples, pears, pineapple, and/or berries), cored (or pitted) and peeled or unpeeled (totally up to you)

3 Tbsp sugar (divided)

3 Tbsp plus 1 tsp light olive oil (divided)

1 ½ cups old-fashioned rolled oats

½ cup roughly chopped pecans, almonds, or walnuts

A good pinch of kosher salt

½ tsp ground cinnamon

1 tsp vanilla extract

½ cup boiling water

SPECIAL TOOLS OR EQUIPMENT

Indoor grill pan or cast-iron skillet

Preheat oven to 375°F.

In a medium bowl, combine fruit and 1 tablespoon sugar and toss to combine. Set aside.

Preheat an indoor grill pan or cast-iron skillet over medium-high heat. Brush 1 teaspoon of olive oil on the pan. Once the pan or skillet is hot, add the fruit and grill about 3 minutes per side, until softened and grill marks appear. If using a grill pan, transfer fruit to an 8- or 9-inch baking dish and set aside. If using a cast-iron skillet, leave the grilled fruit in the skillet and set aside.

In the same medium bowl, combine oats, the remaining 2 tablespoons of sugar, nuts, salt, cinnamon, and vanilla. Pour in the boiling water and stir well. Spoon the topping over the grilled fruit, then drizzle with the remaining 3 tablespoons of olive oil.

Cover with aluminum foil or an ovenproof lid and bake for 10 minutes. Uncover, then bake for another 10 minutes.

Serve warm.

OPTIONAL Quick Fruit Crisp with Oats and Cinnamon can be made in individual ramekins. Follow the recipe above but divide the fruit and topping into 6 ramekins.

STORAGE Quick Fruit Crisp with Oats and Cinnamon can be stored in the refrigerator for up to 3 days or in the freezer for up to 2 weeks.

REHEAT To reheat, bring the fruit crisp to room temperature and heat, loosely covered, in a 375°F oven for 6–8 minutes.

Lemon and poppy seeds make a perfect pairing, but when you add a fudgy-gooey swirl, this cake is next level. It's a guaranteed crowd-pleaser, designed to appeal to cake lovers of all ages.

LEMON–POPPY SEED SWIRL CAKE

READY IN ABOUT 1 HOUR

MAKES 1 (9-INCH) BUNDT CAKE

¾ cup light olive oil, plus extra for greasing

2 cups all-purpose flour, plus extra for dusting

1 cup sugar

3 eggs, room temperature

1 cup orange juice (or ½ cup orange juice + ½ cup lemon juice)

2 tsp baking powder

1 tsp baking soda (divided)

½ tsp kosher salt

½ cup poppy seeds

Grated zest of 2 lemons

1 cup chocolate syrup (such as Hershey's or U-bet), plus extra for drizzling

SPECIAL TOOLS OR EQUIPMENT
Bundt pan

GOOD TO KNOW Room-temperature eggs mix into the batter more evenly, and they also create more voluminous baked goods, which is especially important in a sponge-cake like this one.

STORAGE Lemon–Poppy Seed Swirl Cake can be stored in the freezer for up to 1 month wrapped tightly in plastic wrap.

Preheat oven to 350°F. Grease a 9-inch Bundt pan with olive oil and dust lightly with flour. Shake out the excess flour.

In a stand mixer fitted with the paddle attachment (or using a hand-held mixer), beat olive oil and sugar on medium-high speed for 3 minutes. With the mixer running on medium-high speed, add eggs, one at a time, and mix for 5 minutes. Add the orange juice (or orange-lemon juice) and mix for another minute.

In a large bowl, sift together flour, baking powder, ½ tsp baking soda, and salt. Add the flour mixture to the batter and mix for 1–2 minutes, until combined. Using a spatula, fold in poppy seeds and lemon zest.

Reserve 1 cup of batter in a medium bowl and set aside. Pour the remaining batter evenly into the prepared pan.

To the reserved 1 cup of batter, stir in chocolate syrup and the remaining ½ tsp baking soda. Spoon the reserved chocolate batter into the pan. Using a knife, swirl the chocolate batter into the mixture.

Bake for 50–60 minutes, until the cake springs back when tapped or a skewer inserted into the cake comes out clean. Set aside to cool completely before removing from the pan.

Run a knife along the sides and center of the Bundt pan to loosen the cake from the pan. Invert the cake onto a cake plate or platter and set aside to cool.

Drizzle chocolate syrup on top and serve.

When on vacation in the British Virgin Islands, I was served this pie. I was simply blown away by the idea of a pie baked directly on a regular plate—just hot, caramel apples topped with a flaky, cinnamon-sprinkled crust (in other words, no bottom crust!). This sweet and sticky dessert is best enjoyed with a spoon and eaten directly off the baking dish.

CARAMEL APPLE PIE ON A PLATE

READY IN 40 MINUTES

MAKES 1 (9-INCH) PIE

Light olive oil, for greasing

1 cup dark brown sugar

½ cup (1 stick) butter or dairy-free butter

¼ cup full-fat milk or dairy-free milk (such as coconut, hazelnut, or almond)

1 tsp vanilla extract

Pinch of salt

3 Granny Smith apples, peeled, cored, and very thinly sliced

1 Tbsp cornstarch

½ tsp ground cinnamon

½ tsp sugar

1 sheet puff pastry dough, thawed and rolled out to ¼-inch thickness

1 egg, beaten

Cinnamon sugar, for sprinkling

Confectioner's sugar, for dusting

SPECIAL TOOLS OR EQUIPMENT

9-inch ovenproof ceramic plate or pie plate

Pastry brush

Preheat oven to 400°F. Grease an ovenproof ceramic plate (or pie plate) with olive oil. Set aside.

In a small saucepan, combine brown sugar, butter, and milk and whisk over medium-high heat. Cook for 7–8 minutes, until the mixture is bubbling and has thickened. Remove from heat, then stir in vanilla and salt. Set aside.

In a medium bowl, combine apples, cornstarch, cinnamon, and sugar and toss well to coat.

Return the caramel to the stovetop over low heat. Add the apples and stir to combine. Bring the mixture to a boil, then immediately remove it from the heat.

Spoon the apple-caramel mixture onto the prepared plate. Place the puff pastry over the apples, pinching along the edges to seal the pastry over the edge of the plate. Trim off any excess pastry dough.

Using a sharp knife, cut 4 incisions into the pie crust to create vents for steam to escape during baking. Using a pastry brush, brush beaten egg over the pastry. Sprinkle cinnamon sugar over top.

Bake for 20 minutes, until puffed up and golden. Set aside for 2 minutes to cool.

Dust with confectioner's sugar and serve immediately.

An updated version of "La Pasta" featured in my cookbook *The Modern Menu*, this cake embodies the flavors of my childhood. Every new year, every break of fast, every important milestone, this gorgeous, fluffy cake made an appearance. This taller and lighter version, laced with the subtle flavor of orange blossom, rivals some of the most elegant cakes I've seen and may even be more delicious than the original.

ORANGE BLOSSOM CHIFFON CAKE WITH ROSE PETALS

READY IN ABOUT 1 HOUR

MAKES 1 (9-INCH) CAKE

½ cup neutral oil such as avocado oil, vegetable oil, or rice bran oil, plus extra for greasing

2 cups all-purpose flour, sifted, plus extra for dusting

7 eggs, room temperature

1 ¼ cups sugar

½ cup orange juice

½ tsp orange blossom water

2 tsp baking powder

Pinch of salt

1 tsp edible dried rose petals (see tip below), crushed between your fingers

SPECIAL TOOLS OR EQUIPMENT

Angel food pan

GOOD TO KNOW Edible rose petals are simply dried rose petals and are readily available online, in specialty food stores, and at most farmer's markets. Check the packaging for organically grown roses that are free of sprays and pesticides. And, keep in mind, a little bit goes a long way.

Preheat oven to 325°F. Grease a 9-inch angel food pan with oil and dust lightly with flour. Shake out the excess flour.

In a stand mixer fitted with the whisk attachment (or using a hand-held mixer), beat eggs on medium-high speed for 3 minutes. With the mixer on medium-high speed, slowly add sugar, 1 tablespoon at a time. (It will take about 8 minutes.) The mixture should be thick, glossy, and nearly fill up the entire bowl.

Reduce the speed to medium. Add oil, orange juice, and orange blossom water and mix for 2 minutes. Replace the whisk attachment with a paddle attachment.

In a large bowl, combine flour, baking powder, and salt. Add half of the flour mixture to the egg mixture and mix on medium-low speed for 1 minute. Add the remaining flour mixture and mix for another 1–2 minutes, until well combined. (If you do not have a paddle attachment, you can use a spatula to fold in the baking powder, salt, and flour.)

Pour the batter into the prepared pan and bake for 50–60 minutes, until the cake springs back when tapped or a skewer inserted into the cake comes out clean. Set aside to cool completely before removing from the pan.

Run a knife along the sides and center of the pan to loosen the cake from the pan. Invert the cake onto a cake plate or platter. Sprinkle the crushed rose petals over the cake.

ORANGE BLOSSOM
CHIFFON CAKE WITH
ROSE PETALS

Israeli cheesecake is entirely different from American cheesecake. It is creamy, cool, and sandwiched between a buttery crust and crumb. Unlike other cheesecakes, this style of cheesecake is simple to prepare and requires minimal baking—only the crust and crumbs are baked. It tastes incredible.

ISRAELI-STYLE CHEESECAKE

READY IN 40 MINUTES,
PLUS 4 HOURS CHILLING TIME

SERVES 8–10

CRUST AND CRUMBS

1 ½ cups all-purpose flour

1 tsp baking powder

¼ tsp salt

½ cup (1 stick) unsalted butter, cubed

½ cup sugar

1 tsp vanilla extract

3 egg yolks

CRUST AND CRUMBS Preheat oven to 350°F. Line the base of 2 (9-inch) springform pans with parchment paper (see tip at end). Alternatively, line 1 (9-inch) springform pan and 1 baking sheet.

In a medium bowl, sift together flour, baking powder, and salt. Set aside.

In a stand mixer fitted with the paddle attachment (or using a hand-held mixer), cream butter and sugar on medium-high for 2 minutes. Add the vanilla and egg yolks. Mix on medium speed for 1 minute, until combined.

Add the flour mixture to the wet ingredients. Mix on medium speed until a dough is formed.

Divide the dough into 2 equal-sized balls. Add a dough ball to the prepared pan and, using your fingertips, spread out and press the dough into the base in an even layer. Repeat with the other dough ball in the second baking pan.

Bake both for 20 minutes, until golden. Remove the pans from the oven and set aside to cool completely.

2 cups heavy cream

1 cup sugar

1 tsp vanilla extract or seeds from
1 vanilla pod

3 (8-oz) packages cream cheese,
softened

Grated zest of 1 lemon

SPECIAL TOOLS OR EQUIPMENT

2 (9-inch) springform pans or
1 (9-inch) springform pan and
1 baking sheet

CHEESECAKE FILLING Meanwhile, prepare the cheesecake filling. In a stand mixer fitted with the whisk attachment (or using a hand-held mixer), combine heavy cream, sugar, and vanilla and beat for 5 minutes, until stiff peaks form. (The peaks should stand straight up.) Transfer mixture to a bowl.

Switch to the paddle attachment. Combine cream cheese and lemon zest and mix for 1 minute, until light and fluffy. Add the whipped cream and mix on medium speed until combined. Pour the cheesecake filling into the springform pan. Using a spatula, spread mixture in an even layer.

Using your hands, crumble the crust from the other pan into fine crumbs. Sprinkle the crumbs over top the cheesecake. Cover with plastic wrap and refrigerate for 4 hours or overnight.

To serve, carefully remove the cheesecake from the springform pan, peel away the parchment paper, and transfer to a serving plate.

GET ORGANIZED To line a spring-form baking pan with parchment paper, trace the pan on a piece of parchment paper with a pen or pencil. Cut out the shape. Spray the pan lightly with cooking spray and press the parchment paper into the base of the pan.

MAKE IT AHEAD The crust and crumbs can be prepared in advance, wrapped tightly in plastic wrap, and kept in a cool, dry place for up to 3 days. (Or in the freezer for up to 1 month.)

MAKE IT AHEAD The filling can be prepared up to 2 hours in advance.

Whenever I feel like celebrating (which is often!), this is my go-to cake. It's beautiful, festive, indulgent, and all my favorite flavors in one dessert. (It does my Nutella obsession justice.) If you're not a fan of the hazelnut chocolate spread, you can also top the cake with your favorite jam, preserve, icing, nuts, or even fresh fruit.

CHOCOLATE HAZELNUT CELEBRATION CAKE

READY IN 1 HOUR,
PLUS COOLING TIME

MAKES 2 (9-INCH) CAKES OR
1 (9- × 11-INCH) CAKE

1 cup neutral oil such as avocado oil, vegetable oil, or rice bran oil, plus extra for greasing

1 cup all-purpose flour, plus extra for dusting

1 cup sugar

4 eggs, room temperature

1 cup sour cream

1 tsp vanilla extract

1 cup chocolate drinking powder (such as Nesquik or Hershey's)

¼ tsp ground cinnamon

1 tsp baking powder

Pinch of salt

1 ½ cups Nutella or other chocolate spread (divided)

2 cups chopped roasted hazelnuts (divided)

Preheat oven to 350°F. Grease the cake pan(s) with oil and dust lightly with flour. Shake out any excess flour.

In a stand mixer fitted with the paddle attachment (or using a hand-held mixer), beat oil and sugar on medium-high speed for 3 minutes, until combined. With the motor running, add eggs, one at a time, until well incorporated.

Reduce speed to medium, then add sour cream and vanilla. Mix for 2 minutes.

In a separate large bowl, sift together flour, chocolate drinking powder, cinnamon, baking powder, and salt. Add the flour mixture to the batter and mix for 1–2 minutes, until combined.

Pour batter into the prepared pan(s). (Divide the batter equally between the 2 round cake pans, if using.) Bake for 30–40 minutes, until the cake springs back when tapped or a skewer inserted into the cake comes out clean. Set aside to cool completely before removing from the pan(s).

If using 2 round pans, invert a cooled cake onto a serving plate. Spread about ¾ cup of Nutella on top of the cake. Sprinkle 1 cup of chopped hazelnuts over the Nutella. Invert the remaining cake over the iced cake. Repeat with the remaining Nutella and hazelnuts.

If using a 9- × 11-inch pan, leave the cake in the baking dish and spread a thick and even layer of Nutella on top. Sprinkle with the chopped hazelnuts.

MAKE IT AHEAD Chocolate Hazelnut Celebration Cake (without Nutella and nuts) can be made up to 2 days in advance, wrapped tightly in plastic wrap, and stored in the refrigerator before frosting and assembling.

STORAGE Chocolate Hazelnut Celebration Cake (without Nutella and nuts) can be wrapped tightly in plastic wrap and stored in the freezer for up to 1 month. Defrost overnight before frosting and assembling.

METRIC CONVERSION CHART

VOLUME

IMPERIAL	METRIC
⅛ tsp	0.5 mL
¼ tsp	1 mL
½ tsp	2.5 mL
¾ tsp	4 mL
1 tsp	5 mL
½ Tbsp	8 mL
1 Tbsp	15 mL
1½ Tbsp	23 mL
2 Tbsp	30 mL
¼ cup	60 mL
⅓ cup	80 mL
½ cup	125 mL
⅔ cup	165 mL
¾ cup	185 mL
1 cup	250 mL
1¼ cups	310 mL
1⅓ cups	330 mL
1½ cups	375 mL
1⅔ cups	415 mL
1¾ cups	435 mL
2 cups	500 mL
2¼ cups	560 mL
2⅓ cups	580 mL
2½ cups	625 mL
2¾ cups	690 mL
3 cups	750 mL
4 cups (1 quart)	1 L
5 cups	1.25 L
6 cups	1.5 L
7 cups	1.75 L
8 cups (2 quarts)	2 L
12 cups (3 quarts)	3 L

WEIGHT

IMPERIAL	METRIC
½ oz	15 g
1 oz	30 g
2 oz	60 g
3 oz	85 g
4 oz (¼ lb)	115 g
5 oz	140 g
6 oz	170 g
7 oz	200 g
8 oz (½ lb)	225 g
9 oz	255 g
10 oz	285 g
11 oz	310 g
12 oz (¾ lb)	340 g
13 oz	370 g
14 oz	400 g
15 oz	425 g
16 oz (1 lb)	450 g
1¼ lbs	570 g
1½ lbs	670 g
2 lbs	900 g
3 lbs	1.4 kg
4 lbs	1.8 kg
5 lbs	2.3 kg
6 lbs	2.7 kg

LINEAR

IMPERIAL	METRIC
⅛ inch	3 mm
¼ inch	6 mm
½ inch	12 mm
¾ inch	2 cm
1 inch	2.5 cm
1¼ inches	3 cm
1½ inches	3.5 cm
1¾ inches	4.5 cm
2 inches	5 cm
2½ inches	6.5 cm
3 inches	7.5 cm
4 inches	10 cm
5 inches	12.5 cm
6 inches	15 cm
7 inches	18 cm
10 inches	25 cm
12 inches (1 foot)	30 cm
13 inches	33 cm
16 inches	41 cm
18 inches	46 cm
24 inches (2 feet)	60 cm
28 inches	70 cm
30 inches	75 cm
6 feet	1.8 m

LIQUID MEASURES (FOR ALCOHOL)

IMPERIAL	METRIC
½ fl oz	15 mL
1 fl oz	30 mL
2 fl oz	60 mL
3 fl oz	90 mL
4 fl oz	120 mL

CANS AND JARS

IMPERIAL	METRIC
6 oz	177 mL
14 oz	398 mL
19 oz	540 mL
28 oz	796 mL

BAKING PANS

IMPERIAL	METRIC
5- × 9-inch loaf pan	2 L loaf pan
9- × 13-inch cake pan	4 L cake pan
11- × 17-inch baking sheet	30 × 45 cm baking sheet

TEMPERATURE

IMPERIAL	METRIC
90°F	32°C
120°F	49°C
125°F	52°C
130°F	54°C
140°F	60°C
150°F	66°C
155°F	68°C
160°F	71°C
165°F	74°C
170°F	77°C
175°F	80°C
180°F	82°C
190°F	88°C
200°F	93°C
240°F	116°C
250°F	121°C
300°F	149°C
325°F	163°C
350°F	177°C
360°F	182°C
375°F	191°C

OVEN TEMPERATURE

IMPERIAL	METRIC
200°F	95°C
250°F	120°C
275°F	135°C
300°F	150°C
325°F	160°C
350°F	180°C
375°F	190°C
400°F	200°C
425°F	220°C
450°F	230°C
500°F	260°C
550°F	290°C

ACKNOWLEDGMENTS

To my extremely talented creative team: Kate Sears, Hadas Smirnoff, Paige Hicks, Eric Kjensrud, Spencer Richards, and Naomi Freilich. I am so grateful to have worked with you all.

The Figure 1 Publishing team: Chris Labonte, Michelle Meade, Naomi MacDougall, and Lara Smith. It may have been a crazy time to make a book, but you made it seem easy. Thank you for your trust and patience.

Adeena Sussman: your generous heart and authenticity is what make you who you are. Thank you for your gentle kindness and friendship.

Andrea Burnett: you've been by my side since day one of this cookbook journey. Thank you for everything.

My incredible family and friends, especially the trio who appear in this book: Gealia, Jeanne, and Julie. I am so blessed to be surrounded by amazing people. I appreciate you all so much.

Mom and Dad: Thank you for giving me the tools to listen to my own voice and be proud of who I am, and for showing me the value of hard work. I love you.

Lee and Murray: You've shown me the meaning of true strength. Thank you for all your support.

Milan, Emanuel, Rafi, and Jude: Thank you for being the greatest joys in my life. Of all the creations I've ever worked on, you four are certainly the ones I am most proud of. Locally sourced, sweet and delectable, colorful, and intense with a hint of spice that's hard to kick. Yet no matter how much I've had, I always feel like there's room for one more bite. I love you all.

Milan: I'm proud of you inside and outside of the kitchen. Take it from me— if you can derive immense joy from taking a single bite of food, you can find that happiness in almost anything. Keep that gift safe.

Emanuel: I still don't know what it will take to get you to eat salad, but that's one of the things that makes you who you are. I admire your consistency, your compassion, and your heart.

Rafi: Thankfully, one of you inherited my passion for party planning, organizing, long lists, and bossing those around us! Strong, fierce, and wise beyond your years. You're one of "us," that's for sure. Love you.

Jude: You are the warm sunshine in our lives. Keep shining.

Jon: And lastly, my sous chef in life. Thank you for pushing me to be my best self. You make everyone around you want to be better.

INDEX

Page numbers in italics refer to photos.

A

allspice, in crispy spaghetti pie, 151

ALMONDS

herb salad, lime, and currants, 70, *71*

in nut and honey jars, 98

in quick fruit crisp with oats and cinnamon, 163

roasted, with lemon and thyme, 52, *53*

with sesame seeds and chili powder, 52

anise and sesame tea biscuits, Moroccan, 160, *161*. *See also* fennel; star anise, in nut and honey jars

APPLE(S)

cider vinegar, in mini poke bowls with soy-garlic sauce, 51

pie, caramel, on a plate, 166, *167*

in quick fruit crisp with oats and cinnamon, 163

arayes (grilled stuffed pita), 150

Arctic char with chili, hazelnut, and dill oil, 94, *95*

artichokes and fennel, chicken with, 106, *107*

ARUGULA

and lemon, veal Milanese with, 122, *123*

salad, black olives, black sesame, and citrus, 62

asparagus with eggs, truffle oil, and Parmesan, 144, *145*

AVOCADO

in petite green salad with spicy green tahini, 69

in rice bowls with fish and honey-lime drizzle, 153

B

baby gem with pistachio crumbs, grainy Dijon, and rose petals, 66, *67*

baby yams with saffron cream, 134, *135*

BAGELS

in shawarma salad with za'atar croutons and tahini, 125

for smoked salmon with shallot, dill, and lemon, 84

balsamic glaze, iceberg lettuce, and basil, tomato carpaccio with, 63

BALSAMIC VINEGAR

in balsamic glaze, 63

in chicken with artichokes and fennel, 106

in chicken with red onion and fig sauce, 108

in garlic-confit chicken with lemon and thyme, 102

BASIL

in baby gem with pistachio crumbs, grainy Dijon, and rose petals, 66

in berry frosé, 159

burrata, and mint, grilled peaches with, 64, *65*

in chicken with red onion and fig sauce, 108

in 15-minute herb-crumbed fish, 90, *91*

in honey-lime sauce, 153

iceberg lettuce, and balsamic glaze, tomato carpaccio with, 63

in lemon-pesto chicken with potatoes and red onions, 109

in penne with tomatoes, garlic, and kale, 152

bass with turmeric, carrot, and chickpeas, 93

beans, edamame. *See* edamame

beans, string, in quick pickled vegetable chips, 46

BEEF

in bibimbap, 110, *111*

kefta with edamame and English peas, 120, *121*

leftover, in arayes (grilled stuffed pita), 150

leftover, in crispy spaghetti pie, 151

leftover, in penne with tomatoes, garlic, and kale, 152

leftover, in tortillas with spicy hummus, 151

short ribs, slow-cooked lollipop, 118, *119*

steak, in flatbread with sumac onions, 152

steak with scallions, sesame, and mint, 116

BERRY(IES). *See also* specific berries

frosé, 159

in quick fruit crisp with oats and cinnamon, 163

wine, and chocolate, 158

bibimbap, 110, *111*

biscuits, tea, Moroccan anise and sesame 160, *161*

blackberries, in wine, berries, and chocolate, 158

BLACK OLIVES

arugula salad, black sesame, and citrus, 62

in shawarma salad with za'atar croutons and tahini, 125

black pepper and za'atar, cashews with, 52

BLACK SESAME. *See also* sesame oil; sesame (seeds)

in almonds with chili powder and sesame seeds, 52

arugula salad, black olives, and citrus, 62

in bibimbap, 110

in mini poke bowls with soy-garlic
sauce, 51

in rice bowls with fish and
honey-lime drizzle, 153

in sesame-scallion salmon
cakes, 86

blueberries, in wine, berries,
and chocolate, 158

bok choy, in quick ginger-scallion
soup with mushrooms and
chiles, 35

branzino with lemon, thyme,
and garlic, 88, 89

BREAD. See also bagels;
breadcrumbs

for fried eggplant and jammy
eggs with herb oil,
136–137

for leek and butternut squash
soup, 36, 37

sourdough, grilled, and truffle
honey, whipped chive ricotta
with, 48, 49

for za'atar croutons and tahini,
shawarma salad with, 125

BREADCRUMBS

in baby gem with pistachio
crumbs, grainy Dijon,
and rose petals, 66

in beef kefta with edamame
and English peas, 120

in 15-minute herb-crumbed
fish, 90, 91

in fried grey sole with lemon
and tartar sauce, 92

in veal Milanese with lemon
and arugula, 122

BROCCOLI

charred, frisée, radicchio, and
jammy eggs with creamy
dill dressing, 68

charred, and garlic, 142, 143

in vegetable ramen with
soy-garlic sauce and peanuts,
132

burrata, basil, and mint, grilled
peaches with, 64, 65

BUTTERNUT SQUASH

and leek soup, 36, 37

in vegetable soup with shaved
Parmesan, 34

C

CABBAGE

green and red, cilantro, salted
cashews, and crunchy chili oil,
76, 77

red, in rice bowls with fish and
honey-lime drizzle, 153

CAKE

chocolate hazelnut celebration,
174, 175

lemon–poppy seed swirl, 164, 165

orange blossom chiffon, with
rose petals, 168, 169, 170

CAPERS

for smoked salmon with shallot,
dill, and lemon, 84

in tartar sauce, 92

caramel apple pie on a plate, 166, 167

caramelized fennel, slow-cooked, 139

carpaccio, tomato, with iceberg
lettuce, basil, and balsamic
glaze, 63

CARROTS

in classic kosher turkey, 113–115

in crudités on ice with flaked
salt, 39

in mini poke bowls with soy-garlic
sauce, 51

in quick golden chicken soup, 38

in quick pickled vegetable
chips, 46

in rice bowls with fish and
honey-lime drizzle, 153

turmeric, and chickpeas, sea bass
with, 93

in vegetable ramen with
soy-garlic sauce and peanuts,
132

in vegetable soup with shaved
Parmesan, 34

CASHEWS

cabbage, cilantro, and crunchy
chili oil, 76, 77

in nut and honey jars, 98

with za'atar and black pepper, 52

cauliflower steaks, za'atar, 140, 141

cayenne pepper, in vegetable ramen
with soy-garlic sauce and
peanuts, 132

CELERY

in classic kosher turkey, 113–115

in crudités on ice with flaked salt,
39

in quick golden chicken soup, 38

CHARRED BROCCOLI

frisée, radicchio, and jammy eggs
with creamy dill dressing, 68

and garlic, 142, 143

CHEESE

burrata, basil, and mint, grilled
peaches with, 64, 65

cream cheese, in Israeli-style
cheesecake, 172–173

feta, in leek, lentil, and chickpea
tagine, 148

Parmesan, eggs, and truffle oil,
asparagus with, 144, 145

Parmesan, shaved, vegetable
soup with, 34

ricotta, whipped chive, with
truffle honey and grilled
sourdough, 48, 49

cheesecake, Israeli-style, 171,
172–173

chewy and nutty flourless chocolate
chip cookies, 162

CHICKEN
    with artichokes and fennel, 106,
        107
    crispy, with herbs and white wine,
        105
    in flatbread with sumac onions,
        152
    garlic-confit, with lemon and
        thyme, 102, *103*, *104*
    leftover, in bibimbap, 110, *111*
    leftover, in crispy spaghetti pie, 151
    leftover, in penne with tomatoes,
        garlic, and kale, 152
    lemon-pesto, with potatoes and
        red onions, 109
    with red onion and fig sauce, 108
    in shawarma salad with za'atar
        croutons and tahini, 125
    soup, quick golden, 38
CHICKPEA(S)
    and kale salad with crunchy
        curry dressing, 74, *75*
    leek, and lentil tagine, 148, *149*
    turmeric, and carrot, sea bass
        with, 93
chiffon cake, orange blossom, with
    rose petals, 168, *169*, *170*
CHILE(S). *See also* chili flakes; chili oil
    cayenne pepper, in vegetable
        ramen with soy-garlic sauce
        and peanuts, 132
    dried, in nut and honey jars, 98
    jalapeño and ponzu, seared
        salmon bites with, 80, *81*
    jalapeño, in sea bass with
        turmeric, carrot, and chickpeas,
        93
    jalapeño, in spicy green tahini, 44
    jalapeño, in vegetable ramen with
        soy-garlic sauce and peanuts,
        132
    serrano, and mushrooms, ginger-
        scallion soup with, 35
CHILI FLAKES
    in cabbage, cilantro, salted
        cashews, and crunchy
        chili oil, 76
    hazelnut, and dill oil, Arctic char
        with chili, 94, *95*
    in leek and butternut squash
        soup, 36
    in penne with tomatoes, garlic,
        and kale, 152
    in quick preserved lemon, 99

CHILI OIL
    cabbage, cilantro, and salted
        cashews, 76, *77*
    in vegetable ramen with
        soy-garlic sauce and peanuts,
        132
chili powder and sesame seeds,
    almonds with, 52
chive ricotta with truffle honey and
    grilled sourdough, 48, *49*
CHOCOLATE
    chip cookies, chewy and nutty
        flourless, 162
    hazelnut celebration cake, 174, *175*
    syrup, in lemon–poppy seed
        swirl cake, 164
    wine, and berries, 158
CILANTRO
    cabbage, salted cashews, and
        crunchy chili oil, 76, *77*
    in 15-minute herb-crumbed
        fish, 90, *91*
    in herb salad, lime, almonds,
        and currants, 70
    in honey-lime sauce, 153
    in spicy green tahini, 44
CINNAMON
    in beef kefta with edamame and
        English peas, 120, *121*
    in caramel apple pie on a plate,
        166
    in chocolate hazelnut celebration
        cake, 174
    in crispy spaghetti pie, 151
    and oats, quick fruit crisp with, 163
    sticks, in nut and honey jars, 98
CITRUS. *See also specific citrus fruits*
    arugula salad, black olives, and
        black sesame, 62
    and sage, lamb chops with, 126,
        127
    sliced, with pistachio dust, 156, *157*
    zest, radish, and shallot, tuna
        crudo with, 82
classic kosher turkey, 113–115
CLEMENTINE
    in lamb chops with citrus and
        sage, 126
    in sliced citrus with pistachio
        dust, 156
coffee-rubbed roast, 117
confit, garlic, 99
confit garlic chicken with lemon and
    thyme, 102, *103*, *104*

cookies, chewy and nutty flourless
    chocolate chip, 162
crab, imitation, in mini poke bowls
    with soy-garlic sauce, 51
crackers, in 15-minute herb-crumbed
    fish, 90, *91*
cream cheese, in Israeli-style
    cheesecake, 172–173
creamy dill dressing, frisée, radicchio,
    charred broccoli, and jammy
    eggs with, 68
crème, onion, mashed potatoes
    with, 147
crispy chicken with herbs and
    white wine, 105
crispy mushroom rice, 130
crispy potatoes and onions, 131
crispy-skinned salmon, 83
crispy spaghetti pie, 151
croutons, za'atar, and tahini,
    shawarma salad with, 125
CRUDITÉS
    on ice with flaked salt, 39
    for spicy green tahini, 44
crudo, tuna, with radish, citrus zest,
    and shallot, 82
crunchy chili oil, cabbage, cilantro,
    and salted cashews, 76, *77*
crunchy curry dressing, kale and
    chickpea salad with, 74, *75*
crust and crumbs, for Israeli-style
    cheesecake, 172
CUCUMBER
    in crudités on ice with flaked
        salt, 39
    in kale and chickpea salad with
        crunchy curry dressing, 74
    in mini poke bowls with soy-garlic
        sauce, 51
    in quick pickled vegetable chips,
        46
    in shawarma salad with za'atar
        croutons and tahini, 125
currants, herb salad, lime, and
    almonds, 70, *71*
curry dressing, kale and chickpea
    salad with, 74, *75*

D
Dijon. *See* grainy Dijon
DILL
    dressing, creamy, frisée, radicchio,
        charred broccoli, and jammy
        eggs with, 68

in 15-minute herb-crumbed fish, 90, *91*

in hash browns and eggs, 146

in herb salad, lime, almonds, and currants, 70

oil, chili, and hazelnut, Arctic char with, 94, *95*

shallot, and lemon, smoked salmon with, 84, *85*

in slow-cooked caramelized fennel, 139

in tartar sauce, 92

in vegetable soup with shaved Parmesan, 34

DRESSING. *See also* drizzle; sauces and spreads

creamy dill, frisée, radicchio, charred broccoli, and jammy eggs with, 68

crunchy curry, kale and chickpea salad with, 74, *75*

lemon-za'atar, fennel, pomegranate, and parsley with, 72, *73*

DRIZZLE. *See also* dressing; sauces and spreads

honey-lime, rice bowls with fish and, 153

lime-poppy seed, honeydew with sea salt and, 40, *41*

E

EDAMAME

and English peas, beef kefta with, 120, *121*

in imitation crab, in mini poke bowls with soy-garlic sauce, 51

eggplant, fried, and jammy eggs with herb oil, 136–137, *138*

EGGS

in bibimbap, 110, *111*

and hash browns, 146

jammy, and fried eggplant with herb oil, 136–137, *138*

jammy, frisée, radicchio, and charred broccoli with creamy dill dressing, 68

truffle oil, and Parmesan, asparagus with, 144, *145*

endive, in crudités on ice with flaked salt, 39. *See also* frisée, radicchio, charred broccoli, and jammy eggs with creamy dill dressing

English peas. *See* peas

espresso, in perfect coffee-rubbed roast, 117

everything bagel seasoning, in spicy tuna tartare in roasted seaweed cones, 42

F

FENNEL

and artichokes, chicken with, 106, *107*

in crudités on ice with flaked salt, 39

pomegranate, and parsley with lemon-za'atar dressing, 72, *73*

in quick pickled vegetable chips, 46

slow-cooked caramelized, 139

feta cheese, in leek, lentil, and chickpea tagine, 148

15-minute herb-crumbed fish, 90, *91*

FIG

dried, in nut and honey jars, 98

and red onion sauce, chicken with, 108

FISH. *See also specific fish*

in bibimbap, 110, *111*

15-minute herb-crumbed, 90, *91*

and honey-lime drizzle, rice bowls with, 153

leftover, in penne with tomatoes, garlic, and kale, 152

flatbread with sumac onions, 152. *See also* pita, grilled stuffed (arayes); tortillas with spicy hummus

flavored vodka, 98

flourless chocolate chip cookies, chewy and nutty, 162

fried eggplant and jammy eggs with herb oil, 136–137, *138*

fried grey sole with lemon and tartar sauce, 92

frisée, radicchio, charred broccoli, and jammy eggs with creamy dill dressing, 68

frosé, berry, 159

fruit crisp with oats and cinnamon, 163. *See also specific fruit*

G

GARLIC

and charred broccoli, 142, *143*

in chicken with artichokes and fennel, 106

confit, 99

-confit chicken with lemon and thyme, 102, *103, 104*

in crispy chicken with herbs and white wine, 105

-herb "butter," 113

in honey-lime sauce, 153

lemon, and thyme, branzino with, 88, *89*

-soy sauce, mini poke bowls with, 51

-soy sauce and peanuts, vegetable ramen with, 132, *133*

tomatoes, and kale, penne with, 152

GINGER

in honey-lime sauce, 153

-scallion soup with mushrooms and chiles, 35

in slow-cooked caramelized fennel, 139

in soy-garlic sauce, 132

golden chicken soup, 38

GRAINY DIJON

in arugula salad, black olives, black sesame, and citrus, 62

in chicken with artichokes and fennel, 106

in fennel, pomegranate, and parsley with lemon-za'atar dressing, 72

in frisée, radicchio, charred broccoli, and jammy eggs with creamy dill dressing, 68

pistachio crumbs, and rose petals, baby gem with, 66, *67*

in tartar sauce, 92

grapefruit, in sliced citrus with pistachio dust, 156

green salad, petite, with spicy green tahini, 69

green tahini, spicy. *See* spicy green tahini

grey sole, fried, with lemon and tartar sauce, 92

grilled halibut with marinated onions, 87

grilled peaches with burrata, basil, and mint, 64, *65*

grilled sourdough and truffle honey, whipped chive ricotta with, 48, *49*

grilled stuffed pita (arayes), 150

H

halibut, grilled, with marinated onions, 87

hamburger, leftover, in tortillas with spicy hummus, 151

harissa, in tortillas with spicy hummus, 151

hash browns and eggs, 146

HAZELNUT

chili, and dill oil, Arctic char with, 94, *95*

chocolate celebration cake, 174, *175*

HERB(S). *See also specific herbs*

-crumbed fish, 15-minute, 90, *91*

-garlic "butter," 113

in honey-lime sauce, 153

oil, fried eggplant and jammy eggs with, 136–137, *138*

in rice bowls with fish and honey-lime drizzle, 153

salad, lime, almonds, and currants, 70, *71*

and white wine, crispy chicken with, 105

HONEY

in chicken with red onion and fig sauce, 108

-lime drizzle, rice bowls with fish and, 153

and nut jars, 98

truffle, and grilled sourdough, whipped chive ricotta with, 48, *49*

honeydew with sea salt and lime–poppy seed drizzle, 40, *41*

hummus

in flatbread with sumac onions, 152

spicy, tortillas with, 151

I

iceberg lettuce, basil, and balsamic glaze, tomato carpaccio with, 63

imitation crab, in mini poke bowls with soy-garlic sauce, 51

Israeli-style cheesecake, *171*, 172–173

J

JALAPEÑO

and ponzu, seared salmon bites with, 80, *81*

in sea bass with turmeric, carrot, and chickpeas, 93

in spicy green tahini, 44

in vegetable ramen with soy-garlic sauce and peanuts, 132

JAMMY EGGS

and fried eggplant with herb oil, 136–137, *138*

frisée, radicchio, and charred broccoli with creamy dill dressing, 68

K

KALE

and chickpea salad with crunchy curry dressing, 74, *75*

tomatoes, and garlic, penne with, 152

KEFTA

beef, with edamame and English peas, 120, *121*

leftover, in tortillas with spicy hummus, 151

KETCHUP

in beef kefta with edamame and English peas, 120

in chicken with red onion and fig sauce, 108

kosher turkey, classic, 113–115

L

LAMB

chops with citrus and sage, 126, *127*

leftover, in arayes (grilled stuffed pita), 150

leftover, in bibimbap, 110, *111*

LEEK

and butternut squash soup, 36, *37*

lentil, and chickpea tagine, 148, *149*

LEMON

in arayes (grilled stuffed pita), 150

and arugula, veal Milanese with, 122, *123*

in chicken with artichokes and fennel, 106

in classic kosher turkey, 113–115

in fennel, pomegranate, and parsley with lemon-za'atar dressing, 72

in 15-minute herb-crumbed fish, 90, *91*

in fried grey sole with lemon and tartar sauce, 92

in frisée, radicchio, charred broccoli, and jammy eggs with creamy dill dressing, 68

in garlic confit, 99

for grilled halibut with marinated onions, 87

in Israeli-style cheesecake, 172–173

-pesto chicken with potatoes and red onions, 109

in petite green salad with spicy green tahini, 69

-poppy seed swirl cake, 164, *165*

quick preserved, 99

in sea bass with turmeric, carrot, and chickpeas, 93

shallot, and dill, smoked salmon with, 84, *85*

in shawarma salad with za'atar croutons and tahini, 125

in slow-cooked caramelized fennel, 139

and tartar sauce, fried grey sole with, 92

thyme, and garlic, branzino with, 88, *89*

and thyme, garlic-confit chicken with, 102, *103*, *104*

and thyme, roasted almonds with, 52, *53*

-za'atar dressing, fennel, pomegranate, and parsley with, 72, *73*

lentil, leek, and chickpea tagine, 148, *149*

LETTUCE

baby gem, with pistachio crumbs, grainy Dijon, and rose petals, 66, *67*

frisée, radicchio, charred broccoli, and jammy eggs with creamy dill dressing, 68

iceberg, basil, and balsamic glaze, tomato carpaccio with, 63

romaine, in shawarma salad with za'atar croutons and tahini, 125

LIME

herb salad, almonds, and currants, 70, *71*

-honey drizzle, rice bowls with fish and, 153

-honey sauce, 153

–poppy seed drizzle, honeydew with sea salt and, 40, *41*

in tuna crudo with radish, citrus
zest, and shallot, 82
lollipop short ribs, slow-cooked,
118, *119*

M

marinated onions, grilled halibut
with, 87
mashed potatoes with onion crème,
147
MAYONNAISE
in classic kosher turkey, 113–115
in crispy chicken with herbs and
white wine, 105
in sesame-scallion salmon
cakes, 86
spicy, 42
in tartar sauce, 92
meatballs, leftover, in tortillas with
spicy hummus, 151. *See also* beef:
kefta with edamame and
English peas
meatloaf, leftover, in tortillas with
spicy hummus, 151
mini poke bowls with soy-garlic
sauce, 51
MINT
in arayes (grilled stuffed pita),
150
in baby yams with saffron cream,
134
in berry frosé, 159
burrata, and basil, grilled peaches
with, 64, *65*
in herb salad, lime, almonds, and
currants, 70
in honeydew with sea salt and
lime–poppy seed drizzle,
40, *41*
scallions, and sesame, steak
with, 116
in wine, berries, and chocolate,
158
MIRIN
in ponzu sauce, 80
in soy-garlic sauce, 132
Moroccan anise and sesame
tea biscuits, 160, *161*
MUSHROOM(S)
and chiles, ginger-scallion
soup with, 35
rice, crispy, 130
mustard. *See* grainy Dijon

N

noodles, vegetable ramen with
soy-garlic sauce and peanuts,
132, *133*. *See also* pasta
NUT(S). *See also* almonds; cashews;
hazelnut; pecans; pistachio;
seed(s); walnuts
in chewy and nutty flourless
chocolate chip cookies, 162
and honey jars, 98
peanuts and soy-garlic sauce,
vegetable ramen with, 132, *133*
pine nuts, in leek, lentil, and
chickpea tagine, 148
in quick fruit crisp with oats and
cinnamon, 163
Nutella, in chocolate hazelnut
celebration cake, 174

O

oats and cinnamon, quick fruit
crisp with, 163
OLIVES, BLACK
arugula salad, black sesame,
and citrus, 62
in shawarma salad with za'atar
croutons and tahini, 125
ONION
in beef kefta with edamame and
English peas, 120
in chicken with artichokes and
fennel, 106
in classic kosher turkey, 113–115
crème, mashed potatoes with, 147
in crispy mushroom rice, 130
in hash browns and eggs, 146
marinated, grilled halibut with, 87
in perfect coffee-rubbed roast, 117
and potatoes, crispy, 131
in quick golden chicken soup, 38

red, and fig sauce, chicken with,
108
red, and potatoes, lemon-pesto
chicken with, 109
red, in quick pickled vegetable
chips, 46
in sea bass with turmeric, carrot,
and chickpeas, 93
in slow-cooked caramelized
fennel, 139
sumac, flatbread with, 152
in vegetable ramen with soy-garlic
sauce and peanuts, 132

in vegetable soup with shaved
Parmesan, 34
ORANGE
in Arctic char with chili, hazelnut,
and dill oil, 94, *95*
in arugula salad, black olives,
black sesame, and citrus, 62
blossom chiffon cake with rose
petals, 168, *169*, *170*
in chicken with red onion and
fig sauce, 108
in lamb chops with citrus and
sage, 126
in lemon–poppy seed swirl cake,
164
in Moroccan anise and sesame
tea biscuits, 160
in nut and honey jars, 98
in orange blossom chiffon cake
with rose petals, 168
in ponzu sauce, 80
in sliced citrus with pistachio dust,
156
in slow-cooked caramelized
fennel, 139
in tuna crudo with radish, citrus
zest, and shallot, 82

P

PARMESAN
eggs, and truffle oil, asparagus
with, 144, *145*
shaved, vegetable soup
with, 34
PARSLEY
in arayes (grilled stuffed pita), 150
in beef kefta with edamame and
English peas, 120
in crispy chicken with herbs and
white wine, 105
in crispy potatoes and onions, 131
fennel, and pomegranate with
lemon-za'atar dressing, 72, *73*
in 15-minute herb-crumbed fish,
90, *91*
in garlic-herb "butter," 113
for grilled halibut with marinated
onions, 87
in herb salad, lime, almonds,
and currants, 70
in honey-lime sauce, 153
in leek, lentil, and chickpea tagine,
148
in quick golden chicken soup, 38

in sea bass with turmeric, carrot, and chickpeas, 93

in shawarma salad with za'atar croutons and tahini, 125

PASTA. *See also* ramen, vegetable, with soy-garlic sauce and peanuts

penne with tomatoes, garlic, and kale, 152

spaghetti pie, crispy, 151

PEACHES

grilled, with burrata, basil, and mint, 64, *65*

in quick fruit crisp with oats and cinnamon, 163

peanuts and soy-garlic sauce, vegetable ramen with, 132, *133*

pears, in quick fruit crisp with oats and cinnamon, 163

PEAS. *See also* snow peas, in vegetable ramen with soy-garlic sauce and peanuts; sugar snap peas, in petite green salad with spicy green tahini

and edamame, beef kefta with, 120, *121*

in petite green salad with spicy green tahini, 69

PECANS

in chewy and nutty flourless chocolate chip cookies, 162

in nut and honey jars, 98

in quick fruit crisp with oats and cinnamon, 163

penne with tomatoes, garlic, and kale, 152

perfect coffee-rubbed roast, 117

pesto-lemon chicken with potatoes and red onions, 109

petite green salad with spicy green tahini, 69

pickled vegetable chips, 46

pickled vegetable chips, in bibimbap, 110

pickles, in shawarma salad with za'atar croutons and tahini, 125

PIE

caramel apple, on a plate, 166, *167*

crispy spaghetti, 151

pineapple, in quick fruit crisp with oats and cinnamon, 163

pine nuts, in leek, lentil, and chickpea tagine, 148

PISTACHIO

crumbs, grainy Dijon, and rose petals, baby gem with, 66, *67*

dust, sliced citrus with, 156, *157*

pita, grilled stuffed (arayes), 150

plums, in quick fruit crisp with oats and cinnamon, 163

poke bowls with soy-garlic sauce, 51

POMEGRANATE

fennel, and parsley with lemon-za'atar dressing, 72, *73*

in flavored vodka, 98

pomelo, in sliced citrus with pistachio dust, 156

ponzu and jalapeño, seared salmon bites with, 80, *81*

ponzu sauce, 80

POPPY SEED

–lemon swirl cake, 164, *165*

–lime drizzle, honeydew with sea salt and 40, *41*

POTATOES

in hash browns and eggs, 146

mashed, with onion crème, 147

and onions, crispy, 131

in quick golden chicken soup, 38

and red onions, lemon-pesto chicken with, 109

preserved lemon, 99

puff pastry dough, in caramel apple pie on a plate, 166

pumpkin seeds, in cabbage, cilantro, salted cashews, and crunchy chili oil, 76

Q

quick fruit crisp with oats and cinnamon, 163

quick ginger-scallion soup with mushrooms and chiles, 35

quick golden chicken soup, 38

quick pickled vegetable chips, 46, *47*

quick pickled vegetable chips, in bibimbap, 110, *111*

quick preserved lemon, 99

R

radicchio, frisée, charred broccoli, and jammy eggs with creamy dill dressing, 68

RADISH(ES)

citrus zest, and shallot, tuna crudo with, 82

in crudités on ice with flaked salt, 39

in quick pickled vegetable chips, 46

for smoked salmon with shallot, dill, and lemon, 84

ramen, vegetable, with soy-garlic sauce and peanuts, 132, *133*

raspberries, in wine, berries, and chocolate, 158

RED ONION

and fig sauce, chicken with, 108

in flatbread with sumac onions, 152

marinated, grilled halibut with, 87

and potatoes, lemon-pesto chicken with, 109

in quick pickled vegetable chips, 46

RED WINE

in perfect coffee-rubbed roast, 117

in slow-cooked lollipop short ribs, 118

in wine, berries, and chocolate, 158

RED WINE VINEGAR

in arugula salad, black olives, black sesame, and citrus, 62

in flatbread with sumac onions, 152

in grilled halibut with marinated onions, 87

in quick pickled vegetable chips, 46

ribs, short, slow-cooked, 118, *119*

RICE

in bibimbap, 110, *111*

bowls with fish and honey-lime drizzle, 153

crispy mushroom, 130

in mini poke bowls with soy-garlic sauce, 51

RICE VINEGAR

in cabbage, cilantro, salted cashews, and crunchy chili oil, 76

in kale and chickpea salad with crunchy curry dressing, 74, *75*

in ponzu sauce, 80

in soy-garlic sauce, 132

ricotta, whipped chive, with truffle honey and grilled sourdough, 48, *49*

roast, perfect coffee-rubbed, 117

roasted almonds with lemon and thyme, 52, *53*

roasted seaweed cones, spicy tuna tartare in, 42, *43*

romaine lettuce, in shawarma salad with za'atar croutons and tahini, 125

ROSEMARY

in chicken with artichokes and fennel, 106

in crispy chicken with herbs and white wine, 105

in slow-cooked lollipop short ribs, 118

ROSE PETALS

orange blossom chiffon cake with, 168, *169, 170*

pistachio crumbs, and grainy Dijon, baby gem with, 66, *67*

rosé wine, in berry frosé, 159

S

SAFFRON

cream, baby yams with, 134, *135*

in slow-cooked caramelized fennel, 139

SAGE

and citrus, lamb chops with, 126, *127*

in flavored vodka, 98

in garlic-herb "butter," 113

in vegetable soup with shaved Parmesan, 34

SALAD

arugula, black olives, black sesame, and citrus, 62

baby gem with pistachio crumbs, grainy Dijon, and rose petals, 66, *67*

cabbage, cilantro, salted cashews, and crunchy chili oil, 76

fennel, pomegranate, and parsley with lemon-za'atar dressing, *72, 73*

frisée, radicchio, charred broccoli, and jammy eggs with creamy dill dressing, 68

grilled peaches with burrata, basil, and mint, 64, *65*

herb, lime, almonds, and currants, 70, *71*

kale and chickpea, with crunchy curry dressing, 74, *75*

petite green, with spicy green tahini, 69

shawarma, with za'atar croutons and tahini, 125

tomato carpaccio with iceberg lettuce, basil, and balsamic glaze, 63

SALMON

bites, seared, with jalapeño and ponzu, 80, *81*

cakes, sesame-scallion, 86

crispy-skinned, 83

in mini poke bowls with soy-garlic sauce, 51

smoked, with shallot, dill, and lemon, 84, *85*

salt and lime–poppy seed drizzle, honeydew with, 40, *41*

salted cashews, cabbage, cilantro, and crunchy chili oil, 76, *77*

SAUCES AND SPREADS. *See also* dressing; drizzle

balsamic glaze, 63

garlic-herb "butter," 113

herb oil, 137

honey-lime sauce, 153

ponzu sauce, 80

soy-garlic sauce, 132

spicy green tahini, 44, *45*

spicy mayonnaise, 42

tartar sauce, 92

whipped chive ricotta with truffle honey and grilled sourdough, 48, *49*

SCALLION(S)

in crispy mushroom rice, 130

-ginger soup with mushrooms and chiles, 35

in herb salad, lime, almonds, and currants, 70

in mini poke bowls with soy-garlic sauce, 51

in rice bowls with fish and honey-lime drizzle, 153

sesame, and mint, steak with, 116

-sesame salmon cakes, 86

in spicy tuna tartare in roasted seaweed cones, 42

in vegetable ramen with soy-garlic sauce and peanuts, 132

sea bass with turmeric, carrot, and chickpeas, 93

seared salmon bites with jalapeño and ponzu, 80, *81*

sea salt and lime–poppy seed drizzle, honeydew with, 40, *41*

seaweed cones, roasted, spicy tuna tartare in, 42, *43*

SEED(S). *See also* nut(s); sesame (seeds)

poppy, –lemon swirl cake, 164, *165*

poppy, –lime drizzle, honeydew with sea salt and, 40, *41*

pumpkin, in cabbage, cilantro, salted cashews, and crunchy chili oil, 76

sunflower, in cabbage, cilantro, salted cashews, and crunchy chili oil, 76

sunflower, in kale and chickpea salad with crunchy curry dressing, 74

serrano chile, in quick ginger-scallion soup with mushrooms and chiles, 35

SESAME OIL

in cabbage, cilantro, salted cashews, and crunchy chili oil, 76

in mini poke bowls with soy-garlic sauce, 51

in ponzu sauce, 80

in quick ginger-scallion soup with mushrooms and chiles, 35

in soy-garlic sauce, 132

in spicy tuna tartare in roasted seaweed cones, 42

SESAME (SEEDS). *See also* sesame oil

arugula salad, black olives, and citrus, 62

in bibimbap, 110, *111*

in cabbage, cilantro, salted cashews, and crunchy chili oil, 76

and chili powder, almonds with, 52

in mini poke bowls with soy-garlic sauce, 51

in Moroccan anise and sesame tea biscuits, 160

in rice bowls with fish and honey-lime drizzle, 153

-scallion salmon cakes, 86

scallions, and mint, steak with, 116

SHALLOT

dill, and lemon, smoked salmon with, 84, *85*

radish, and citrus zest, tuna crudo with, 82
in slow-cooked lollipop short ribs, 118
shaved Parmesan, vegetable soup with, 34
shawarma salad with za'atar croutons and tahini, 125
shiitake mushrooms and chiles, in quick ginger-scallion soup, 35
short ribs, slow-cooked lollipop, 118, *119*
sliced citrus with pistachio dust, 156, *157*
slow-cooked caramelized fennel, 139
slow-cooked lollipop short ribs, 118, *119*
smoked salmon with shallot, dill, and lemon, 84, *85*
snow peas, in vegetable ramen with soy-garlic sauce and peanuts, 132
sole, fried grey, with lemon and tartar sauce, 92
SOUP
    ginger-scallion, with mushrooms and chiles, 35
    leek and butternut squash, 36, *37*
    quick golden chicken, 38
    vegetable, with shaved Parmesan, 34
sour cream, in chocolate hazelnut celebration cake, 174
sourdough, grilled, and truffle honey, whipped chive ricotta with, 48, *49*
SOY (SAUCE)
    -garlic sauce, mini poke bowls with, 51
    -garlic sauce and peanuts, vegetable ramen with, 132, *133*
    in honey-lime sauce, 153
    in ponzu sauce, 80
    in quick ginger-scallion soup with mushrooms and chiles, 35
spaghetti pie, crispy, 151
SPICY GREEN TAHINI, 44, *45*
    for fried eggplant and jammy eggs with herb oil, 136–137
    petite green salad with, 69
spicy hummus, tortillas with, 151
spicy mayonnaise, 42
spicy tuna tartare in roasted seaweed cones, 42, *43*
SPINACH
    in bibimbap, 110, *111*

in petite green salad with spicy green tahini, 69
squash. *See* butternut squash; zucchini
Sriracha, in spicy mayonnaise, 42
star anise, in nut and honey jars, 98
STEAK
    in flatbread with sumac onions, 152
    with scallions, sesame, and mint, 116
strawberries, in wine, berries, and chocolate, 158
string beans, in quick pickled vegetable chips, 46
stuffed pita, grilled (arayes), 150
sugar snap peas, in petite green salad with spicy green tahini, 69
sumac onions, flatbread with, 152
SUNFLOWER SEEDS
    in cabbage, cilantro, salted cashews, and crunchy chili oil, 76
    in kale and chickpea salad with crunchy curry dressing, 74
swirl cake, lemon–poppy seed, 164, *165*

T
tagine, leek, lentil, and chickpea, 148, *149*
TAHINI
    spicy green, 44, *45*
    spicy green, for fried eggplant and jammy eggs with herb oil, 136–137
    spicy green, petite green salad with, 69
    and za'atar croutons, shawarma salad with, 125
tangerine, in sliced citrus with pistachio dust, 156
tartare, spicy tuna, in roasted seaweed cones, 42, *43*
tartar sauce and lemon, fried grey sole with, 92
THYME
    in classic kosher turkey, 113–115
    in crispy chicken with herbs and white wine, 105
    in garlic confit, 99
    in garlic-herb "butter," 113
    in leek and butternut squash soup, 36, *37*

lemon, and garlic, branzino with, 88, *89*
and lemon, garlic-confit chicken with, 102, *103*, *104*
and lemon, roasted almonds with, 52, *53*
TOMATO(ES). *See also* ketchup
    in arayes (grilled stuffed pita), 150
    carpaccio with iceberg lettuce, basil, and balsamic glaze, 63
    garlic, and kale, penne with, 152
    paste, in crispy spaghetti pie, 151
    paste, in slow-cooked lollipop short ribs, 118
    in shawarma salad with za'atar croutons and tahini, 125
    in slow-cooked lollipop short ribs, 118
    for smoked salmon with shallot, dill, and lemon, 84
tortillas with spicy hummus, 151
TRUFFLE
    honey and grilled sourdough, whipped chive ricotta with, 48, *49*
    oil, eggs, and Parmesan, asparagus with, 144, *145*
TUNA
    crudo with radish, citrus zest, and shallot, 82
    tartare, spicy, in roasted seaweed cones, 42, *43*
TURKEY
    classic kosher, 113–115
    in crispy spaghetti pie, 151
    in shawarma salad with za'atar croutons and tahini, 125
TURMERIC
    carrot, and chickpeas, sea bass with, 93
    in classic kosher turkey, 113–115
    in crispy potatoes and onions, 131

V
veal Milanese with lemon and arugula, 122, *123*
VEGETABLE. *See also specific vegetables*
    chips, quick pickled, 46, *47*
    chips, quick pickled, in bibimbap, 110, *111*
    ramen with soy-garlic sauce and peanuts, 132, *133*
    soup with shaved Parmesan, 34
vodka, flavored, 98

W

WALNUTS
in chewy and nutty flourless
chocolate chip cookies, 162
in quick fruit crisp with oats and
cinnamon, 163
whipped chive ricotta with truffle
honey and grilled sourdough, 48,
49
WHITE WINE
in classic kosher turkey, 113–115
and herbs, crispy chicken with, 105
in lamb chops with citrus and sage,
126
wine. *See* mirin; red wine; rosé wine,
in berry frosé; white wine
Worcestershire sauce, in tartar
sauce, 92
wraps, whole-wheat, in tortillas with
spicy hummus, 151

Y

YAM(S)
in quick golden chicken soup, 38
with saffron cream, 134, *135*
in vegetable soup with shaved
Parmesan, 34
YOGURT
in baby yams with saffron cream,
134
Greek, in frisée, radicchio, charred
broccoli, and jammy eggs with
creamy dill dressing, 68
Greek, in herb salad, lime,
almonds, and currants, 70
in leek, lentil, and chickpea tagine,
148

Z

ZA'ATAR
and black pepper, cashews with, 52
cauliflower steaks, 140, *141*
croutons and tahini, shawarma
salad with, 125
in herb salad, lime, almonds, and
currants, 70
-lemon dressing, fennel,
pomegranate, and parsley with,
72, *73*
ZUCCHINI
in leek, lentil, and chickpea tagine,
148
in vegetable soup with shaved
Parmesan, 34